Getting Rich on
Any Income

Getting Rich on Any Income

81 Ways to Increase Your Wealth—Even If You're in Debt

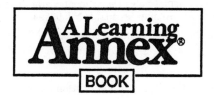

Jeffrey Gomez

A Citadel Press Book
Published by Carol Publishing Group

A Citadel Press Book
Published by Carol Publishing Group
Citadel Press is a registered trademark of Carol Communications, Inc.
Editorial Offices: 600 Madison Avenue, New York, N.Y. 10022
Sales and Distribution Offices: 120 Enterprise Avenue, Secaucus, N.J.
  07094
In Canada: Canadian Manda Group, P.O. Box 920, Station U, Toronto,
  Ontario M8Z 5P9
Queries regarding rights and permissions should be addressed to
Carol Publishing Group, 600 Madison Avenue, New York, N.Y. 10022

Carol Publishing Group books are available at special discounts for
bulk purchases, for sales promotions, fund raising, or educational
purposes. Special editions can be created to specifications.
For details contact: Special Sales Department, Carol Publishing
Group, 120 Enterprise Avenue, Secaucus, N.J. 07094

Manufactured in the United States of America

10 9 8 7 6 5 4 3 2 1

Library of Congress Cataloging-in-Publication Data

Gomez, Jeffrey.
    Getting rich on any income : 81 ways to increase your wealth—even if
you're in debt / Jeffrey Gomez
        p.   cm.
    "A Learning Annex book."
    "A Citadel Press book."
    ISBN 0-8065-1519-8
    1. Finance, Personal.   2. Investments.   I. Title
HG179.G672   1994
332.6—dc20   93-44223
                                                                           CIP

Contents

Introduction

A New Way of Living

Many of us have been brought up to spend money like water! The pervasive "easy come, easy go" attitude has created a society in debt, making us dependent on loans, credit, and most of all, that golden paycheck at the end of the week.

Those who are finally secure realize this attitude truism does not help them maintain their lifestyles. Rather, they have learned to live within their means by adjusting their habits in some fundamental ways. Poor or middle-class people who wish to become financially secure can do so by taking several different paths. A scant few are lucky. Anyone can hit a jackpot at a Las Vegas casino, or win a multi-million dollar lottery. Many follow through on a dream or idea that catches on. But wealthy people have climbed the corporate ladder or built a business into a contemporary success story. What virtually all rich people have in common is a relentless drive to accumulate money. To do so, each one of them had to create a new way of living. This "attitude adjustment," and the secret facts behind creating wealth for *yourself*, are the subject of this book.

There are at least eighty-one ways to increase your wealth in this book. Not every idea presented here is for everyone. (Rest assured, if you follow only one or two of the tips this book has to offer, you can save yourself hundreds of dollars per year!) But there *are* dozens of hard and fast facts designed to save you money, build a stockpile of cash, and open opportunities for you to invest your newfound wealth in lucrative markets. As you use this book, you will find lots of new "clothing" to "try on" and "model" for yourself.

Whatever ideas appeal to you, by adopting the values of rich people you are guaranteed—no matter what your current salary—to learn how to create your own wealth.

The specific references and resources cited in this pages form a specific strategy for all of us who yearn to be rich.

1. Recognize your personal attitudes toward spending and make a decision to leave behind "bad programming."
2. Examine how those with wealth conduct their day-to-day lives, and learn how you can follow their lead.
3. Assess how modern society throws stumbling blocks in your path that may keep you from attaining wealth.
4. Learn how to take control of the system and make it work *overtime* for you.
5. Get yourself out of debt, and learn how to avoid debt in the future.
6. Initiate a plan to generate money and create wealth with low risk at high yield.

Unfortunately, we are all taught by television and the movies to view the rich as idle, glamorous, and awash in luxury. We are led to believe that they know something we don't. As you will see, this is just not true!

Wealthy people value money the same as the rest of us. In fact, they are reluctant to part with cash unless they can be certain that prices are as low as possible and quality is guaranteed. Rich people will always choose a bargain over a convenience, and they will use every resource at their disposal to find those bargains. In this age of information, these very same resources are available to you, and they are as easy to find as libraries and as accessible as local circulars and newspapers.

In fact, the gathering and proper use of information is so important to creating wealth that a veritable philosophy can be made of it. *Getting Rich on Any Income* will outline this philosophy for you and incorporate its use through facts and illustrations covering nearly every facet of daily life.

Using this book, you will learn how to:

- avoid being ripped off by convenience stores and spot legal ways you can be robbed of your hard-earned cash
- throw away the "pacifiers" that society gives to the poor to keep them in line
- save thousands every year by cutting your telephone, entertainment, travel, research, grocery, and credit card bills by at least half
- avoid having coupons cost you money instead of saving it
- save 50 percent to an astonishing 80 percent by buying in bulk or getting things wholesale through the mail
- barter your skills and services for whatever it is you need without spending a cent
- slash costs and still have quality health care, medicine, and eyeglass or contact lens prescriptions
- save big money on expensive consultants and accountants by taking advantage of tax-free services and business support
- make the stock market, mutual funds, variable annuities, and investment frontiers create wealth for you

One thing is certain. Living rich requires you to make a commitment to change. Fortunately, this need not be a painful process! Small adjustments in the way you spend your money and the way you perceive the world around you can help you to start building wealth rapidly. In turn, this can lead to a better standard of living for us all.

Part I
How the Rich Live

1 | *Lifestyles of the Rich*

Getting Beyond the Glamour

The French call the elegance and beauty of the fabulously wealthy *glamour:* suntanned skin, luxurious furniture, fancy clothing, and priceless baubles. This is the "face" the rich wear on countless magazine covers, nighttime soap operas, and television screens reproducing such syndicated fodder as *Lifestyles of the Rich and Famous.* But if we trace the word *glamour* back to its medieval origins, we may find a way into that metaphorical door which separates people with money and security from those who are sorely in debt!

In the tales of King Arthur and his Knights of the Round Table, the evil sorceress Morgan le Fey created a *glamour* around the sweet Nimwe so she could lure the magician Merlin into a trap, leaving the good king bereft of his chief advisor. Evil witches and warlocks used *glamour* spells to deceive their victims, dazzling them with seductive beauty and sparkling treasures before emptying their pockets or stealing their souls.

Glamour is good to look at, but it is also inherently artificial. It shows us something charming, but it is really a distraction. So long as you know this, feel free to enjoy the fleeting beauty. Truly believe in what the glamour is showing you, and you will remain a poor person indeed!

This is not to say that wealthy people don't have mansions and yachts. The benefits of having lots of money are many, as anyone who has ever visited a rich aunt or uncle's home will tell you. But what you never get to see on old *Dynasty* or *Dallas* TV reruns is the purchase of those mansions and yachts for the lowest prices negotiable!

Men and women who work hard to amass their wealth respect and appreciate every single one of their dollars. They are *frugal*. That particular characteristic is never mentioned in the society gossip columns nor is it portrayed on television—mostly because it's not terribly exciting. But it is a fact of their lives. They are very careful about what they spend.

Think about this; because soon you are going to have to make a choice. A sort of reverse glamour has been placed around frugality. We call people who refuse to take taxis "tightwads," people who count pennies at supermarkets "misers." To be called a "Scrooge" in our culture is tantamount to damnation! Hollywood celebrities who aren't seen in designer clothes tossing their money around at posh parties are held suspect, or worse, are not written about at all.

TV and print advertising, fashion trends and the latest fads, our obsession with food and dieting, everything implores us to spend. And we are actually made to feel guilty if we don't. Of course a stigma is placed on being frugal—if you aren't spending your money as soon as it gets into your pocket, how can everyone else make money off you?

People who get wealthy and stay wealthy are aware of this vicious cycle and have found many ways around it. They recognize the fact that much of our media exists for the sole purpose of selling us things—at top dollar, no less. Everyone loves a big spender, and the true mega-rich are content to let the Donald Trumps and Elizabeth Taylors feed the glamour machines with lavish lifestyles they themselves downplay while they are asking questions, gathering knowledge, keeping track of all of their assets, and staying abreast of every opportunity. Most of all, they are being frugal.

Ultimately, the decision is yours. Any number of the recommendations in this book will save you a substantial amount of money. But adopting the philosophy and tactics espoused here as a whole may make you rich. This, however, requires a change in how you look at the media, listen to the opinions of your friends and family, and view the *spend-spend-spend* attitude of society. It will require you to leave behind your old notions about how you treat your money and to take on the financial values of the undisputed specialists in this particular field—the rich. Your alternative is simply to continue running that rat race, pockets empty, and to accept as a fact of life big debt and a meager savings account.

And by the way, you are going to get there without breaking a single law or bruising any of your moral tenets. That's a promise.

Poor Is the Past

The first step in establishing a different personal attitude toward handling money and wealth is to break away from preconceived notions about spending. Far too many of us spend money, in amounts both small and large, without thinking twice about price, value, or quality.

We don't question what it is we're buying! We groan about inflated costs, but we don't haggle or take our business elsewhere. None of us wants to rock the boat. We substitute niceness and gentility for driving a hard bargain, even in places like car dealerships and electronics stores, where making a deal is expected by the salesmen.

That ever-present glamour programs us to skim the surface and take what is up front, instead of digging for the real value hidden somewhere in back. Not only do we pay for the product, but we pay for the packaging, the sales staff, rental for the venue, the window dressing, and even the enticing little advertisement that got us there in the first place!

Flashy commercials and neon signs, an endless stream of "buy it" noise bombards our senses everywhere we go. Like the zombies wandering aimlessly through the shopping mall in George Romero's *Dawn of the Dead*, we are frazzled consumers, scooping cash out of our wallets and purses as if spending were some sort of involuntary act, like blinking or breathing. A loaf of bread at a bakery can cost about 49¢. At the 7-Eleven next store, a "processed" and "super enriched" loaf of the same weight goes for $1.69. Why then do we shamble into that darned 7-Eleven and shell out *more than three times* the value of the bread? Because we have been stupefied!

Spending is not one of our survival instincts, but we have been programmed to spend money this way since we were old enough to be put down in front of a television set. This has to stop. The rich don't spend money this way. You'd be surprised at all the alternatives there are to top-dollar spending. Many of these are outlined in this book. In any event, you are going to have to learn to recognize these old, ingrained habits and let them go. Wake up! Leave your poor person's attitude in the past, where it belongs.

A New Set of Values

The question arises, if I let go of all my old approaches to money and spending, what do I do to fill the vacuum? Well, there's an old saying: If it looks like a duck, walks like a duck, and quacks like a duck, then it's a duck!

Taking this cue, it really doesn't matter what your current income is. It doesn't matter how much you have in your savings account, or even how far in debt you've gone. If at this very moment you start to take on the values of a wealthy person, you will, without a doubt, grow wealthier. While the cash may be generated in small increments at first, watch how fast it accumulates as you stick to your guns.

You have already taken the first step in learning how to recognize all those expensive bells and whistles, the "glamour" of the top-dollar hard sell, as well as how being frugal has gotten a bum rap in our society. Now let's take a look at some of the other values one might attribute to a person who is wealthy.

Wealthy people ask questions. They do not allow themselves to be led around by the nose. The reason why they know a good deal when they see it is that they are not afraid to ask pointed questions to learn about what it is they're buying. They know how to determine the best price and quality for their money.

Wealthy people are patient. They sit still long enough for prices to come down. They walk out on negotiations. They take the following year's release of a new model car, giving the manufacturer time to assess its initial performance and fix all the bugs. Contrary to the popular notion, rich people do wait.

Wealthy people gather information and use it. Be it a telephone plan, college for their kids, a method of travel, or a new coffee machine, they will research, compare, and contrast before loosening their purse strings. Impulse purchases are often verboten.

Wealthy people work hard. Well, we all do, but rich people are not afraid to be inconvenienced. As you will soon see, this is one of their greatest secrets. They are meticulous about keeping track of their money and how it is being spent. They are not afraid to go the extra mile, skip over the 7-Eleven for the bakery, or wait until morning if that bakery happens to be closed.

Wealthy people respect and emulate other wealthy people. They stay in touch with those who have similar values, and they benefit from knowing and being with them. They network, keeping their ears and minds open for new deals and fresh perspectives. They give to one another, bartering their skills and striking mutually beneficial agreements. Yes, they are often competitive, but just as often they will follow one another's lead.

Each of these values or rules will be expanded upon in detail later in this book. You will learn how to question and when to be patient. You will be given dozens of leads on researching information, and tips on how to network and rub elbows with the wealthy, as well as how to avoid "conveniences" that ultimately cost you money.

The thing to do right now is to decide to make these rules your own by using them on a daily basis. As a result, you will find yourself becoming more aware of your spending habits and better able to do something to improve them. Your "evil twin" who buys on impulse and allows so many of your hard-earned dollars to fly into other people's coffers, will be stopped once and for all.

Your Personal Vision of Wealth

As the old adage says, you need money to make money. And the faster you circulate your own money, the faster it will grow. Before you can invest, however, you must accumulate a certain amount of wealth to invest. Barring the lottery or the last will and testament of a loving, rich relative, this means you are going to have to set some goals, create a plan, and stick to it.

"Oh, no!" you say. "Here comes one of those dreaded 'D' words, as in *diet, deprivation, discipline,* or *drudgery.*"

Well, how about a "V" word? Creating a vision of yourself as a happy, wealthy person is paramount to becoming one. Lie back and take your time. Imagine yourself rich, not just materially, but emotionally. What kind of person are you going to be when you are rich? What will your relationships be like? How will your home be decorated?

Now that you have imagined yourself as a rich person you have begun the process of eliminating your past as a poor person. If you draw a straight line between yourself now and your wealthy self in the future, you have a road you can walk, jog, or sprint on as quickly (or slowly) as you like.

Does all this seem a little esoteric? It really isn't. Right now, you have a vision of yourself as a rich person. To realize that vision, you are going to have to do a series of concrete things. And because you are not rich already, those things are going to have to start with a fresh approach to handling your own money. Will it take dieting? Will you have to have discipline? Well, how badly do you want to live rich?

If you are determined to change your lot in life, if you want to be wealthy badly enough, the dreaded "D's" won't matter a hoot. There won't be time. You're going to be pursuing your vision of living rich as if someone had built a fire under you; as if your life depended on it.

2 | *Cost Control*

Assessing Your Current Wealth

Having decided to leave behind your casual attitude toward the way you spend money and incorporate into your life the spending and saving attitudes of the rich, it is time to take inventory. Leave no stone unturned. Make a list of all your assets: bankbooks, checkbooks, IRA's, stocks, bonds, CD's, Christmas funds, piggy banks, rainy-day stashes, everything. Bring it all together and prepare to write it down in a way you are going to understand in the future. You don't have to be an accountant, and you don't have to list things in a ledger book. Just use something that you can keep discreetly, like a notebook you can tuck away or a computer file, and start adding things up.

If you like, you may also make a list of your valuables: jewelry, real estate, antiques, and other things that will appreciate in years to come. But set that list aside. For our purposes, we will be dealing with liquid assets, or assets that can be turned into cash with relative ease.

Next, you must bring yourself up to date. All checkbooks must be balanced. You must assess current stock and mutual fund values and apply those values to what you have. An exact dollar equivalent has to be applied to all your liquid assets as of today! Know where each of these books, certificates, and papers, the coins and cash, are located, and make a commitment to keeping track of how everything is doing on a weekly basis by checking newspaper listings or your bank's activity.

Sum up your totals and think about what you've got. Don't get depressed! You are looking at the past, and the future starts right now.

Choose to make a commitment to updating this total as often as possible, daily, weekly, whatever you can be sure you can stick to. No matter what your salary or income, no matter how slightly these figures fluctuate, you have worked hard to earn this money, it belongs to you, and it is worthy of being counted to the last penny.

Every Penny Counts

We have all laughed at that crotchety old cartoon character Scrooge McDuck as he sits amidst mountains of cash and coins counting every penny over and over again. So-called penny-pinchers have been the butts of jokes and objects of derision for centuries. These misers are wide-eyed and drooling, hunchbacked and cackling, lost in a sea of greed and often portrayed as downright villainous—they are not creatures we want to emulate.

But you and I both know that you are not any of these things. To have the vision and drive to want to become rich is no sin. To be focused and thorough it is not necessary to become obsessed or to develop antisocial tics. You have every right to know exactly what belongs to you at any given time. The matter is a private one which needs to be thoroughly understood by you.

When you were a small child, a nickel, a quarter, even a penny was viewed as something precious. A tiny handful of personal responsibility. You went to the store and exchanged these coins for wonderful things, for bubblegum balls or comic books. It is time to regain, if not that sense of wonder, at least that sense of appreciation. That sense of value. There are still a few gumball machines left in the world. Every penny counts.

Be Debt Free

We are living in a society that goes out of its way to put us in debt. Being in debt is one of the fundamental elements that keeps you from living rich. It is how "the club" keeps its golden gates closed, how the wealthy keep us poor. Even teenagers are in debt these days! The cycle of spending and owing is dizzying; it addles us and turns us into anxiety-ridden compulsive spenders. People are lost in debt, forced to worry about it, lose sleep over it, do desperate things about it. Some even drown in it. There is no choice—you must get rid of debt!

First, you must assess what you owe. Gather together all your bills. Everything. Next month's rent, the total tally on your credit cards, totals on payments for the car or house, taxes, school. Don't invent bills you are going to have to pay in the future; just tally up your debt as of today. Among your bills you'll most likely find charge-card bills, mortgages, and different payments known as "buy now, pay later" plans.

You must immediately develop a plan to deal sanely with these bills. Here are some hints.

Stop Throwing Money at Your Problems.

It is entirely too common a solution. People who are distracted, depressed, or anxious in some way tend to spend money thoughtlessly. We are "cheered up" by indulgence, be it with food, new clothes, larger power tools, etc.

But when you think about this, what is really going on is that you are masking your problems, treating the symptoms while blithely ignoring the causes. This keeps you isolated and troubled. What's worse, it keeps you poor. Apply to a friend, relative, clergyman, or inexpensive councilor at your local hospital or community assistance center, and talk it out.

Stop using credit right now!

Once you realize "buy now, pay later" is a trick to stop you from ever being wealthy, it should be a simple matter to recognize this habit and cut it out. The average credit-card holder cannot resist temptation, and may be thousands of dollars in debt at any given time. Credit cards make it easier to buy things you don't really need. They keep infomercials and home shopping channels in business. Most of them charge you ghastly fees just for the privilege of spending your own money. Throw your credit cards away!

If you must wean yourself slowly instead of going cold turkey, at the very least use credit such as American Express, which you are forced to pay at the end of the month. There are a few select cards that do not charge annual fees, such as Discover, which is a bit more acceptable. Also, many credit-card services will wave annual fees if you call to remind them what a good customer you've been. If they don't at this point, threaten to switch to another card! Watch for premiums such as frequent-flyer miles, and avoid holding your credit cards with the same bank where you keep your savings or checking account. Under certain circumstances the bank can pull payment from these accounts to settle credit-card debts!

Finally, you are entitled to one TRW report on your personal credit record per year. Contact TRW Credit Service's free Consumer Assistance hotline by dialing 800-682-7654. They can also answer any of your personal credit questions and even launch investigations if you feel you have been denied credit unjustly. For more information on correcting the blots on your TRW report, you may also write their National Consumer Relations Center, 12606 Greenville Ave., Box 749029, Dallas, Texas 75374.

Pay up all the "little" bills.

Do not let cable bills, electricity, subscriptions, tabs, and other small debts accumulate. These are the bills you can most likely afford to pay today. Why wait until they become unwieldy a few months down the road? Clean them up!

If you can't pay your larger debts right now, break them down and pay them off as quickly as possible.

Your creditors want the money badly enough to listen to reason. It costs big money to hire collection agencies or send lawyers after you; that's why you get so many warnings before any legal action is taken. Contact your creditors before they contact you. Call to let them know you would like to break down your payments, and tell them you will be sending the money on a weekly basis (if at all possible) until the debt is settled. You may also be able to negotiate your debt down. Call your creditors and offer to settle for 50¢ on the dollar. You'll be surprised how many will accept.

Avoid bankruptcy and seek help.

Bankruptcy is ugly, demeaning, and leaves permanent scars on your credit records and in the records of your debtors. Bankruptcy will also not forgive outstanding taxes, child support, alimony, debts accrued under false pretenses, and student loans.

If it seems to you that you have a debt no honest man or woman can be expected pay, it is time to seek some professional help. Pick up the phone and call Debtors Anonymous at 212-642-8222. They can put you in touch with your local chapter or help you with your problem over the phone. Debtors Anonymous will be able to assist you in a variety of ways, without judging or haranguing you.

If your debts are tied specifically to credit, contact the National Foundation for Consumer Credit at 800-388-2227. Someone there can advise you on a particular debt situation.

Slash Spending

In assessing your debts and comparing them to your liquid assets, it will almost certainly become clear that you are spending too much money. Cutting down on spending will give you the dual benefit of being able to pay off your current debts more quickly and to start up savings. Will this require you to lower your standard of living? Well, this book is *not* called *Getting Poor on Any Income!*

Life is too short to deprive yourself of the things you enjoy. Wealthy people are extremely cost-conscious, but they live well and they don't deny themselves for the sake of retaining their wealth. They know enough to look beyond the glamour and find the things they want for the lowest possible cost. They figure out ways to slash spending in every facet of their lives—without their food tasting any worse or their clothes looking any shabbier—and they avoid debt like the plague.

In the next chapter, we will outline some of the many ways cash can be stolen out of your pocket all day long. Once you are aware that this is happening, you will have dozens of opportunities to slash spending, cancel your debts, and start stockpiling cash!

3 | "Convenience" Is Robbing You Blind!

What a Difference a Day Makes

To put it bluntly, most of us are running around like chickens with our heads cut off. We get up in the morning and blindly rush to work, tossing off dollars every step of the way. We pay for gas and tolls or mass transit, coffee and bagels or donuts, maybe a pack of cigarettes and the morning paper. We throw in a snack during the coffee break, and lunch time is split between the corner sandwich shop or diner and buying sundries for the house. Then it's homeward bound, more tolls or tokens, perhaps a stopover at the neighborhood convenience store for eggs and a pint of ice cream.

What people fail to realize is that a *heavy price* is exacted for all this hurrying. When you drink a cup of coffee at home, for example, those few spoonfuls of ground java, a couple of scoops out of the sugar bowl, and the ounce or two of milk you use cost you a grand total of under 10¢. That same cup bought at a neighborhood coffee shop will run you between 45¢ and a dollar, depending on where you work. That's a mark up of between 450 percent and 1000 percent!

Of course, you do get a surly growl from the cashier and an environmentally incorrect Styrofoam cup for all that extra money, but is it really worth it?

Big business has realized that treating the symptoms of

society's ills can be a lot more lucrative than finding a cure. Creating services and products which "save you time" so that you can get to work by nine, cut down on kitchen work, or spend more hours with your loving family has become a multibillion-dollar enterprise. And yet, didn't we all get along just fine before the advent of the all-night convenience store?

24-Hour Thievery

To put it bluntly, the later the place is open, the more horrendously overinflated the prices are going to be. Somebody somewhere caught on that you will dish out double the cash to satisfy that sweet tooth or pick up that forgotten box of disposable diapers in the middle of the night. Does it cost a business more to stay open late? Probably. Do you have to take on those added costs by patronizing it? Absolutely not! Not if you do something big business never counts on: Clear your mind and plan ahead!

Why is it that you don't have the time or forethought to purchase any item at the lowest possible price? Aside from relationships and sex, the biggest concern of the average person is...money! If you are worried about the almighty dollar, what are you doing in that all-night grocery store paying $2.09 for a $1.29 quart of orange juice? The prices quoted in this book will vary from region to region, but you get the point: The differences really are enormous. And when you learn about some of your alternatives, you will realize that this kind of moonlight gouging amounts to nothing short of thievery.

Use the following tactics to make certain these Slurpee-slinging scoundrels never take another penny from you:

1. **Plan ahead.** No one knows your life better than you, so figure out what you're going to need for days (or even weeks) in advance and shop for

those items at the least expensive supermarket in
your area. Take those midnight cravings into
consideration. You can buy a two-week supply of
crisp nachos and hot pepper Velveeta for the price
of one of those oily, wilted, cardboard tubs you'll
get at Store 24.

2. **Take it with you!** Candy bars, sodas, veggies, tea
   bags—impulse purchases amount to hundreds of
   millions of dollars in profit a year for the
   convenience store industry. Save yourself
   hundreds by wiping out the expense of the
   impulse purchase. Be aware of what you might
   want at one point or another during the day. Buy
   these items at supermarkets or discount houses.
   Stock up ahead of time, and you will have the
   perfect excuse to stay out of convenience stores,
   where you are liable to spend at least a hard-
   earned buck on the *National Tattletale* just for
   nosing around.

3. **If you have to, at least compare.** Emergencies do
   come up, but even if you must patronize a
   convenience store, it pays to have the proper
   information at hand. Which is cheaper, Harry's
   Midnight Mart two blocks away, or Yung-Soo's
   Deli on Main? If it's the deli, walk the extra block.
   It's good exercise, and you're showing Harry that
   you're not so lazy as to part with more than you
   have to.

If Harry's is the only all-nighter for miles, don't just
wander in and grab the nearest package of whatever it is
you're looking for. Compare! A manufacturer can impose a
price on an item that the store management cannot legally
adjust. A half gallon of Tide liquid laundry detergent has to
go for $3.99, because that's what is printed on the label. The

same-sized bottle of Bold sitting next to it will probably have the manager's price of $5.99 on it! Prices on any item can have a wide range at convenience or "discount" drug stores.

Lunch

Believe it or not, our culture is one of the only ones that seems to frown on brown bagging it. In Japan and Europe, workers pack their snacks, beverages, and lunches in attractive containers and take them everywhere. These people know that the real convenience is in planning their needs and having their food with them to enjoy at any time in any place. An office-bound luncheon can just as easily become a picnic.

In the heart of the average American city, the ordinary lunch costs around $8. Even if your costs are lower, you are spending between $120 and $160 a month for the privilege of someone else slapping two slices of bread around a pretty shabby piece of meat. Think of what that money can buy at your grocer's delicatessen! Think about how much cash you could raise if you'd simply switch from restaurants and fast food joints to good old fashioned home preparation!

Time spent in line to pay double, triple, even quadruple what a meal would have been worth had you made it at home, will be better spent doing just that. Work it into your routine while watching TV or talking on the phone. You would be surprised at what a source of pride this can be. Afraid your friends and co-workers will have a chuckle at your expense? Well, you'll have the last laugh when you bank (at the very least!) an extra $720 to $960 a year for your efforts.

And remember, these last figures were arrived at just by cutting lunch-time spending in half. What if you could quarter your costs? What if your partner did the same? Your kids? That's thousands of dollars! Do some research. Figure the math out on your own, then decide. Besides, Rubbermaid is making some great looking portable food containers these days.

Finally, if you simply *must* take the occasional meal at a restaurant, seek the least expensive eateries in any area in which you'll be spending time. Compare menus and avoid fast food joints, and don't order in. Check out the places where the locals go; the food ought to be good, and the prices should be reasonable.

Poverty in a Pretty Package

The people who invented microwave ovens are plenty wealthy, but they cannot possibly hold a candle to the multibillionaires who are currently manufacturing foods packaged in microwavable containers. There is no disputing the quickness and convenience of microwaves. Let's hear it for progress! But paying close to a dollar for a six-ounce plastic sealed cup of Beef-a-roni, when the same amount of money can buy enough spaghetti to feed a family of four makes you want to scream.

"I know! I know!" the slimy young corporate hotshot must have said. "Everybody's weight-conscious and in such a hurry, why don't we cut up the food into teeny-tiny portions and put it into these neat, neon-colored packages. We'll give them slick names like *Lunchables* and put thick plastic lids and pull-tabs on them. Heck, I'll bet people will pay through the nose for something like that!"

Remember, pudding packs, disposable drink boxes, those lurid double-tray snacks (one side has the cookie-cracker, the other side has the cheesy-dunk), or just about any product that contains smaller "individually wrapped" products are all priced far beyond the value of the food you are actually taking home to consume.

It is important to remember that this is no diatribe against tasty snacks and microwavable fare. You don't have to give up on the food, just don't give into the marketing.

We saw what happened when you planned ahead and skipped the convenience-store circuit. Now imagine the additional cash you can save (and divert to making yourself wealthy) merely by taking action on the following tips.

1. **Don't get suckered by a pretty face.**
   Manufacturers are counting on your getting so caught up in the newness of the product, the flashiness of its packaging, and its time-saving convenience that you will either overlook or swallow the extra cost. This is especially true when it comes to items aimed at children and teenagers. Remember what we learned about glamour. Don't allow yourself to be seduced into poverty.

2. **Break what you like into components and buy them fresh in bulk.** A box of powdered chocolate pudding will generate a snack pack's worth of desserts for mere pennies a cup.

   Prices plunge when you purchase a lot of something, or when you have to supply the cooking or the container. Buy and store pasta, deli products, potato chips, fruits, and vegetables; prepare them to your taste, then snack on them when you like. (A fringe health benefit here: You will be missing out on all those strange chemicals they use to squeeze and preserve the food in those tiny packages!) Stop seeing preparation as work and start seeing it as savings.

3. **Assemble your own array of reusable storage devices.** Whether it's high-tech burping plasticware or basic aluminum foil and cellophane, you have an inexpensive army of food

and drink preservers at your command. A lot of
the new plastic is interestingly designed, with
separate compartments built in, or thermal
gimmicks included. Toss a pile of penny saltines
on one side and a five cent gob of peanut butter
on the other, and bank the 50¢ you've saved!

A helpful hint: If your food storage containers look
appealing, decorative, or "cool," then you will be more
likely to stick with them, neighbors and co-workers will be
less likely to wrinkle their noses, and the young ones won't
get hassled as much in school.

"Pacifiers"

Ever since we stopped sucking our thumbs we have been
searching for something soothing to put into our mouths. It
truly is an excitable world, but isn't it interesting that so
many of the "thumb replacements" society has created for us
are addictive? Caffeine, nicotine, alcohol, sugar, narcotics—
it is as if big business wants to find your weakness and
create a built-in guarantee that you will keep coming back
to its product.

These substances wake us up in the morning, calm us
after a run-in with the boss, make it a little easier to
socialize at dance clubs. But they are also enervating,
unhealthy, mind-dulling, and worst of all for our purposes,
expensive! Why don't we sit down and try to figure out what
we spend on these various "pacifiers"?

- **Coffee**—We have already seen the abominable
  mark-up coffee is given whenever you buy it
  outside of a supermarket. If you are buying one 45¢
  cup, five days a week, 50 weeks out of a year, you
  are spending $112.50. Now multiply that by two or
  three. How many people drink only one cup a day?
  And double that if your partner or spouse dips into

the java as well. Are you blowing hundreds of
dollars a year on *coffee?*

Office coffee pools can save you money, but
bringing in a thermos of the stuff made to your
own specific taste, or cutting down altogether will
save you more (and probably be more satisfying).

- **Cigarettes**—As taxes and surcharges spiral ever
higher, smoking has become our most expensive
bad habit. Outside of duty free shops and nifty
sales promotions, a name brand pack of coffin nails
will cost you in the neighborhood of $2. Half a
pack a day? $365 a year. Pack a day? $730 a year!

The purpose of this book is not to harp on
health issues, but you must face facts: Cutting
down on smoking can raise cash! And that is the
cash you are going to need to make yourself
wealthy. Nicotine gum, the "patch," and hypnosis
are all pricey ways to quit. Will power is free, and
so is information from the American Cancer
Society, 261 Madison Ave., New York, New York
10016; or the American Lung Association, 1740
Broadway, New York, New York 10019.

- **Alcoholic beverages**—It is a little-known fact that
wealthy people tend to spend less on liquor. This is
because they know how to get it free or on the
cheap! Parties, luncheons, casinos, art openings—
free drinks are offered to respected attendees at all
of these. In addition, people with money know that
getting drunk is an impairment, an easy route to
shutting down the possibilities offered in the
environs. They drink to be sociable and keep their
ears open for potential clients, deals, or
connections. Why shouldn't you?

Outside of dropping the purchase of alcoholic beverages

altogether (thereby saving yourself thousands of dollars in the long run), here are a couple of other helpful hints:

1. **Use your local beverage distribution center.** You can save up to 50 percent of the cost of a case of beer (or soda, or ice) if you seek out and patronize discount houses that usually service local bars, grocery stores, and catering houses. And,

2. **Tip generously!** Bartenders are more likely to use a heavy hand or give you "buy backs" (free drinks) if you surprise them with a big tip on the first round you order. Rich people have impressed many a business client using this technique.

- **Narcotics**—Whether store-bought like aspirin or back pain pills, prescription-bought like Valium, or illegal like marijuana or cocaine, drugs are an expense you might seriously consider living without. Narcotics are mind-numbers. They induce either sleep or spending, neither of which is helpful for gathering wealth. Seek natural (read "free") alternatives, cut down, stop, or, at the very least, mooch them from friends. Turn to Chapter 9, "Health," for information on how to save big money on medicine and prescriptions.

- **Soda, candy, and munchies**—The richest man in America is named Mars, as in almond bars and M&M's. He's made billions off our collective sweet tooth, as have those warring gargantuas Coca-Cola and Pepsi-Cola. We are a nation with the munchies, popping open bags of popcorn and Fritos and feeding ourselves mechanically in front of the TV set.

     This is a form of slavery! We are kept from mounting a mutiny because we are gorged and running on sugar highs! Be honest and tally up what you spend on this stuff in one year; and don't forget to include what goes on while you're watching television. If you're anywhere near the average, the results should be staggering.

Here are a few hints on slashing your spending on these oral "pacifiers":

1. **Cut it all in half.** You've already pledged to keep out of convenience stores, so when you buy only half the junk food you'd ordinarily consume, that's what you are stuck with until the next time you go shopping.

2. **Let your tongue tell you when to stop.** Wake up and be more aware of what it is you're putting into your mouth. The human tongue is naturally sensitive to extremes in sweetness and saltiness. At a certain point it will actually "go numb" as your taste buds overload on the sugar or salt. Do not wait until you are full. Candy and munchies are not made to satisfy hunger; they are made for you to enjoy! When you stop tasting what you are putting into your mouth, stop eating it.

3. **Find something else to do.** People eat junk because they are bored, depressed, angry, lonely, or tired. Replace expensive colas and chips with seltzer and fresh veggies. Find something to do with your hands. Better yet, talk to a friend, figure out what's bothering you, and take immediate action to remedy the problem.

You won't find all that much junk food in a wealthy person's pantry. Their bars may be well stocked, but the bottles can go untouched for months at a time.

These products are not helping you, and many of them can easily become a hindrance. For a wide range of reasons, those who have successfully pursued wealth avoid indulging themselves with most of these "pacifiers." Perhaps you should too! They contribute nothing substantial toward your pursuit of the good life.

The Telephone

As with anything used on credit, taking the telephone for granted will add up to one of your least necessary expenses. We call friends, family members, and lovers two or three times a day just to shoot the breeze. We dial information while our *Yellow Pages* gathers dust in the hall closet. We throw out money-saving information included with our phone bills as if it were junk mail.

While it is true that wealthy people use the telephone like the rest of us, it is the *way* in which they use this important communication device that makes them different. Rich people know that telephones are tools, and tools are ultimately there to make money:

- They prevent conversations from meandering by keeping their calls short and to the point.
- They never pay for a call that, with a bit of research, can be made free of charge.
- They try to be on the receiving end of more calls than they dial out.
- They correspond by other, much less expensive means.

Here is a list of some of the ways in which wealthy people slash spending on telephone bills and still make the most out of their communications. Following any number of these tips will save you significant amounts of money, which can be put to better use elsewhere.

1. Spend 29¢ instead of $29. While no one can argue with the pleasure of hearing a loved one's voice over vast distances, the price this can exact in the long run can be devastating. Keep long-distance phone calls short, sweet, and infrequent; write a letter instead!

Phone calls are ephemeral. They come and go, and fade from memory. A letter is a tangible object, to be held, cherished, perhaps kept forever. Writing makes promises concrete, stories repeatable verbatim. Five pages, front and back, full of musings, anecdotes, clippings, thoughts, and concerns, enclosed in a business-size envelope and sent through the mail for 29¢ is perhaps the greatest bargain the government has to offer. Don't worry about your writing skills or technique. If you just write the way you speak, your correspondent will get the message.

2. Organize your thoughts before you pick up the phone. If the telephone is a tool, learn how to use it to maximum effect. Why are you calling this person? What points will you have to cover before hanging up? What are you giving this person by calling him or her? What do you want in return? These questions may sound cynical at first glance, but think about it. What is wrong with knowing exactly what you are doing, especially when you are spending money doing it?

When you jot down a list on a pad of paper or establish a little mental agenda before you call someone, you are creating a way to use your time and money to their greatest potential. You are benefiting the person you're talking with, because you'll be speaking more clearly and concisely. There will be less of the boring niceties and beating around the bush. Also, you are benefiting yourself by getting the job done more quickly, saving cash, and moving on.

Note: A truly frugal person will actually take advantage of beepers, answering services, voice mail, or even answering machines by leaving the briefest of messages to be called back. Do so at your own discretion.

3. Learn how your phone system works and exploit it. Since the breakup of AT&T, telephone companies have become highly competitive and offer products and services you can take advantage of, depending on your situation. Do a little research. Who and where do you call most often? Watch out for short-term gimmicks that can sucker you into switching before prices shoot back up. Look at the various companies' long-term policies, what times of the day discounts are greatest, and switch to the one that best serves your needs.

Study your monthly phone package closely. Premiums on your kinds of calls may be offered and should be utilized. Also, check the bills themselves for errors, especially if you run a business. Glitches and mistakes in billing that go unnoticed can cost you hundreds of dollars a year. If you find an error, like a charge on a call you didn't make, report it to the phone company and it will be deducted from your bill.

Pesky prefixes like 900 numbers can be blocked by requesting your local phone company to prevent them from being dialed out of your phone. Lose those psychic friends, look up your own recipes and horoscopes, and fantasize with the next heavy breather who calls you up.

4. Never pay for information that is available to you free of charge! The 411 or 555-1212 numbers exist to make phone companies easy cash. Dialing information is the lazy person's way of using the phone book, a way of tossing a couple of quarters out the window.

The telephone company is required by law to give you a set of *White* and *Yellow Pages* free at your request. Use them, if only to spite these people! Phone books from outside your geographical area can often be attained at very low cost by contacting phone companies in areas you know you'll be calling. In some regions, dialing information from a pay phone may be done free of charge.

A tougher economy has led many businesses across the country to offer ways to contact them free of charge. By dialing the national toll-free information service at

800-555-1212, you may inquire whether the company you are looking for has a toll-free consumer line.

You can also send for the *AT&T Toll-Free Consumer Directory*; it lists over 50,000 toll-free telephone numbers, ensuring that you will never have to pay again for a call to a hotel, travel agency, or many other businesses. The current edition costs $9.95 (plus tax and shipping), and you can order it by calling The Sourcebook, 800-451-2100.

5. Use the new telecommunication technologies. These days those high-tech computer hacker types call 29¢ surface mail "snail mail," since telephone lines can deliver vast quantities of information so much more quickly. Facsimile machines and "E-mail" can be used to zap letters, documents, even photographs over great distances cheaply in seconds.

Look into a modem for your computer or an inexpensive quality fax machine for your phone. But the savings will be felt only if you don't get hooked on all those online computer services that come with modems. And avoid those super-inflated fax costs at convenience stores; $2 to send two pages anywhere in 30 seconds is a rip-off.

Periodicals

There is no reason why you should ever have to pay cover price for any publication, particularly newspapers and magazines. Here's an insight into the economics of periodical publishing: When a daily, weekly, or monthly goes to press, it is already paid for. Advertising and subscriptions make up virtually the entire cost of production, salary, and distribution, which means that sales on the stands are gravy!

Every newspaper needs to raise its circulation because it forces the advertisers to continue paying tens of thousands of dollars to reach all those readers. This is one reason why periodicals offer such low subscription rates, and that's why you should take advantage of them.

There is a reason *Sports Illustrated* is one of the top-selling magazines in the world (besides the swimsuit issue). Take a look at the subscription offers in their television commercials. You are being asked to pay up to 50 percent off the cover price of a magazine that costs $3 on the newsstand! And pick up those annoying cards that are always falling out of popular magazines between September and November. These annual subscription drives can save you up to 70 percent off the retail price of many of them! Assemble a list of the ones you really want but won't be able to borrow from the job or flip through at a friend's house. Then, go for it!

There are also subscription services such as American Family Publishers (yes, the company with that big yearly sweepstakes; contact them at 800-237-2400), whose sole job is to keep magazine circulations high by offering tremendous subscription discounts. Remember, don't go in looking for *Cosmo* and come out with *Harper's*, *McCall's*, and *Vanity Fair* as well. As with any sale, the savings is only there if you stash the cash after you've gotten what you set out to get. Leave the rest alone.

Entertainment

You work hard all week and you are doing what it takes to save money. It stands to reason you want to enjoy yourself on your time off, but entertainment spending seems to be the logical area to focus on if you want to cut the fat from your budget. Well, you don't necessarily have to be less entertained in order to spend less money having fun! Let's see how wealthy people approach their leisure time.

Wealthy people are entertained by learning. There can be no argument: The more you know, the richer your life becomes, the greater your potential for becoming cash rich. These people read voraciously. They borrow books, subscribe to magazines, watch cable TV (but won't pay for premium channels they don't use *a lot*), attend lectures and seminars, and so on, all at minimal cost. Open your mind, and hundreds of opportunities will start flowing your way.

Wealthy people enjoy quality entertainment. Museums, zoos, botanical gardens, public parks, and libraries provide inexpensive locales for surprisingly excellent entertainment. As public services, these institutions will often provide forums for classical, jazz, and even popular music, excellent prints of contemporary and classic films, plays, readings of poetry and prose fiction, symposiums on aspects of nature and the environment, travelogs and special exhibits.

You pay for most of these things by making a nominal donation, far less than the cost of a ticket for something similar at a private theater or concert hall. Get over your ingrained, school-trained prejudices against these places and try them. You may find something (or even someone) that will change your life.

Wealthy people enjoy culture and the arts. Cultural and ethnic centers or events can put you in touch with worlds of diversion and entertainment. If you aspire to wealth, it is important for you to become worldly. Exposing yourself to the aspirations and experiences of your own and other cultures will expand your sphere of knowledge and open your mind to ideas that otherwise would be alien to you.

As you will see in Part Three of this book, learning to appreciate culture is like learning a new language: It will give you access to areas from which you would have ordinarily been excluded. For example, a Shakespeare play performed free of charge in an open park can offer you and a date a lovely evening's entertainment. But it also has the potential to bring you into conversation with Bard afficionados at a cocktail party or business luncheon.

You've already talked up the soaps or the football game at the water cooler. Now try Puccini or Miles Davis with someone in the board room. Live a richer life by opening yourself up to the culture and entertainment enjoyed by the rich.

4 | *Poor People Own Everything!*

America the Salesman

Instead of playing a concentrated game of chess with big business, we are all taught to shoot a losing game of craps. Advertising and the media would have us run out and purchase the biggest, brightest, and newest as each item comes on the market. We are compelled to buy a product and remain loyal to it, at least until something "new" and "improved" comes along. The jingles, the catch phrases and the celebrity endorsements, tell us "you gotta get it," and we absently whisper right back at the screen, "I gotta have it."

The mark of good salesmanship is the ability to convince people that they must buy something they don't really need. An even better salesman will sell it to you at twice the going rate. What poor people wind up with are homes cluttered with K-Tel this, Ronco that, and a year's supply of that miraculous spray-powder hair you're supposed to squirt onto your head.

Think about your struggling friends and neighbors. Isn't it interesting that these people have literally tons of stuff? Gizmos, gadgets, knick-knacks, the latest, the hottest, last year's latest and hottest, it goes on and on.

Why is it, that when you visit wealthy people's homes or see them in magazines or TV profiles, their houses seem so

spare, uncluttered, almost spartan? Are their housemaids
that good? Is it all that closet space?

The Stigma of Ownership

One of the biggest leaps to truly living rich on any income
is the realization that you don't need to be saddled with
junk. Wealthy people have self-esteem. They set high standards for themselves and the products and services they
purchase. At the same time, they simply will not be fooled
by the hard-sell, and will go elsewhere or do without it
before paying top dollar. This attitude eliminates nearly all
impulse purchases.

For the rich, every item bought is a valued addition to the
home, cherished and placed there with care. Luxury items
such as electronic equipment, vehicles, jewelry, art, antiques, and furniture are thoroughly researched for du-
rability, longevity, versatility, and quality of construction.
*The rich would rather have a very few nice things than
many shabby things, and this is what distinguishes them.*

The shift in attitude you need to make may not be as big
as you think. In order to live rich, you do not need to stop
buying things altogether and bank your bucks. You need to
treat yourself to the finest—at the lowest possible cost. To
do this, first of all you are going to have to take a good strong
look at the concept of *needing*; it is not wanting to own
everything you see.

"I want it all, and I want it now!" It's a chant that floats in
our collective subconscious. It keeps our garages, closets,
and attics full, and our bank accounts empty. Imagine how
terrified those mega-corporations would be if we all decided to follow a different mantra. You don't have to own
everything. (You don't even have to own it to have it, as we
soon shall see!) In fact, if you were to place a stigma on
ownership, making ownership the last thing you want to do

with a product or service, watch what happens. Suddenly, there is a subtle, and highly potent, shift in power. You become the boss. You take control.

Patience Yields Big Savings

"How could I have ever lived without that?" Well, you did, didn't you? And five will get you ten, if you wait out the impulse to pick up the latest doodad, you can probably continue to live without it in the future.

Patience is more than a virtue; it places you in the driver's seat and can save you tens of thousands of dollars. A person who is patient, asks questions, and doesn't appear too eager is an anomaly to a salesman. Patient people seem to have nothing to lose by walking out of the store empty-handed— a store owner's worst nightmare! When you are patient, you can go anywhere with your own agenda, your own price range, and take command. You have nothing to lose, because your attitude is that whatever it is, you can live without it. Place yourself in a situation where you can negotiate and watch those prices start to tumble!

Here are some pointers on how to apply patience to avoid paying top dollar on just about anything.

1. Wait for a big sale—or find one. Having a sale is a company's tactic for luring buyers into the store—buyers who will pick up several other products on impulse in addition to the item on sale. Don't fall for this! Get in there, browse if you must, then get what you need, and get out of there. Examine local newspapers, penny savers, and even periodicals from other communities in your area for sales on the things you know you need. If necessary, call the store, and make certain the item you're looking for is still available. When a sale hits, go and retrieve your just rewards and bank the difference!

2. Keep on the lookout for the "sell-through." Often,

new products are priced substantially lower than established comparable products so that initial sales can skyrocket. This practice is called "pricing to sell-through" and
is used to create a fanfare, build confidence in the product,
and make a quick buck. This is how a thick hardcover book
can hit the stands and be marked down 25 percent on day
one, or a certain compact disc can be priced at $10.99 when
so many others cost $15. Those of us with kids might recall
how Nintendo dropped the cost of its basic unit dramatically a few years back. It caused a feeding frenzy, and now
we're all stuck paying through the nose for all these games.
Disney uses sell-through to grab the number-one slot on
videocassette sales and break its own records every year!

Take advantage of sell-through if you really want the item
in question and don't forget to use the rebate offers these
things often enclose. Prices will only go up after the fanfare
dies down.

3. Wait for prices to drop. The opposite of sell-through
occurs when a manufacturer believes demand will be so
great for a product that a high price will not deter sales. If
demand is so great, why shouldn't a hefty tag be placed on
the supply? Well, being "first on the block with the new
toy" is something we've all decided to leave in the past
along with poverty—right?

Once you have gotten over this stampede mentality, you
might find after some time that you really don't even need
this product. On the other hand, if you decide the item still
has merit, it is quite possible you'll be rewarded for your
patience with a somewhat saner price.

Take movies, for example. A hot new action flick would
cost a family of four over $30 to go see at a first-run theater.
Four to six months later it's $2.50 at the corner mom-and-
pop video store. If that picture was a klunker (and you are
your own best critic), you've saved yourself at least $27.50.

4. Roll-out models, "cutting-edge" technologies, and

new, "improved" systems are expensive and full of bugs.
Cut through the hype and realize that "new and innovative"
is only so until next year. Technologies are developing so
rapidly that expensive items like cars, stereos, and computers are becoming archaic in months. Where did "beta"
cassettes go? Will digital audio-tape systems catch on?

Those of us on the cutting edge can often get nicked in
the wallet, and there's nothing worse than dragging a
$2,000 item up into the attic "for when Jamie gets a little
older." Go to knowledgeable people and ask questions.
Everyone is biased, so go to several. Find an appropriate
copy of *Consumer Reports* (at the library) and take notes.
Like natural selection, the strongest and fittest will outline
the fads and trends. The wealthy know this, and will wait
patiently for the perfect acquisition.

5. Do not rely on advertising alone. The most stunning
savings and the most amazing bargains will not necessarily
be advertised to the general public. Wholesale outlets,
foreclosures auctions, thrift shops, and stores off the beaten
path rarely take out television or print advertising. As you
will see in Chapter 5, there are many places where real
killings can be made. And though they might never admit it,
those places are where wealthy people may be found
browsing and buying at huge savings. Read on! And remember, you've stopped shooting craps and started playing
chess.

Don't Buy It—Borrow It!

Think about the various "collections" you have laying
around the house. Books, videos, CDs, audiocassettes, cos-
tume jewelry, porcelain figurines: What percentage of these
things do you truly prize? Which ones are valued as
important references and sensory experiences you want to
review over and over? Which ones did you pick up because

"it was hot at the time" or "the cover looked good"? You are wasting money if what you are buying gathers dust from disuse. Here are some alternatives:

Use the best "free" bookstore around. There is a place close to your home where you can find the latest best-sellers, excellent mysteries, endless rows of dictionaries and other reference works, even music and videos on cassette. Go there, show them some ID, take whatever you want, and enjoy it at home for more than enough time to take it all in. This place is called a *public library*, and the best thing about it is that when you've finished with what you've taken, you can put it back there—so it doesn't clutter up your house!

Rent it. We all know how video stores have saved families small fortunes (and saved us the anguish of spending so much on what is so often so little), but fewer people seem to know that so much else is for rent. Carpet and furniture cleaners, floor sanders, paper shredders, computers, VCRs, wheelchairs, business equipment, anything you can think of is rentable. Check rental listings in your local *Yellow Pages*. Why purchase a hugely expensive product that you are only going to use for one special occasion or a couple of times a year?

Relieve a friend of it. If you don't have to own it, then it doesn't matter where you get it from, so long as it's agreed you are going to give it back sometime. From a cup of sugar to a new record you'd like to sample, what are friends and neighbors for? Items become currency if they are swapped, and anything that substitutes for cash is good as far as this book is concerned. Remember, however, the best way to borrow is to offer something *first*. This can range from saying something nice to bartering an item or service in return.

Incidentally, while "duping" (the practice of duplicating

an audio or video recording) is usually regarded as illegal and cannot be condoned, there are legal ways of cutting costs way down on these things. Many of the larger record stores have started the practice of legally creating cheap personalized audiotape "mixes" of favorite songs. This circumvents paying $75 for five compact discs which contain a total of seven listenable tunes. Your video store eventually won't need all ten copes of the latest Kevin Costner movie. Get friendly with the manager and reserve a previously viewed copy at up to 80 percent off the original price. They'll even exchange it for you if the tape looks worn out when you get it home.

Take what you collect seriously. When it comes to placing something on a shelf in your home, take a cue from the wealthy: Put something there that really matters to you, something in which you can take personal pride, and do not allow yourself to part with a dime for anything else.

Think about the kinds of things you keep buying. Make a list of criteria for actually spending money on an item. If it's a CD, for example, then you have to be crazy about at least five songs on the album. If the item does not meet your standards, but you feel you'd still like to enjoy it, then find some way to borrow it.

5 | *Bargains*

Tracking Them Down

We have all been envious of a friend or relative who managed to snare some kind of breathtaking accessory at an impossibly low price. Then there are all those obnoxious, ritzy types who always seem to grab high-ticket items "for a song," claiming "it was a steal!" Scratching our heads, we sullenly accept their explanation: "I was *so* lucky!" Of course, they're lying.

Wealthy people will go to great lengths to avoid being outwitted by sales glamour. Targeting bargains is one of the main ways they get wealthy, and they know keeping costs low is the primary way to stay wealthy. At the same time, they won't scrimp on quality. Buying something cheap that falls apart on you is tantamount to buying it twice, and that's a sin! This requires a little research, a little patience, and a little adventure, but the result is a tremendous pay-off.

Here are some of the things you will need to hunt down bargains:

• **Local "penny-saver" publications.** They are often inserted in your Sunday newspaper or can be found stuck in your mail box or apartment lobby. Chock-full of leads, coupons, and promotions, they are worth closer study. Watch out for expiration dates and check with stores to make certain the item you want is still available.

• **Community publications.** Newspapers, newsletters, and magazines designed to service neighborhoods have always been tools for businesses attracting local patrons. Special prices may be included in these periodicals which may not be available to "outsiders."

• **Classifieds.** How many pieces of virtually untouched exercise equipment have been sold for 50 percent to 90 percent off original cost? Tons! Take advantage of other people's impulse purchases, New Year's resolutions, and whims by scouring the classified sections in various publications for all kinds of bargains.

Of course, here more than most places it pays to know a lot about what it is you are buying. Bring along an expert and don't be afraid to ask dozens of questions. Remember, you can afford to live without it a while longer, and cash up front means any price can be dropped a little bit more.

• **Spy networks.** Your chances of finding bargains increase dramatically when you bring fellow bargain-hunters in on the case. Let friends and relatives know exactly what it is you're looking for. Do not be distracted by the flotsam and jetsam they turn up! You are mining for a precious metal of a specific nature, and running off on tangents to take advantage of bargains you don't need will wind up costing you more than you would have saved. Help your friends find something they're looking for and ask that they return the favor when your time comes.

• **Plotting your course.** Get a map. Contact the source of the bargain and ask for exact instructions on how to get there. If it costs you the difference in gas, food, tolls, and body armor to reach the bargain, you're not saving any money. Resolve not to be distracted by other sales or baited by impulse purchases. This is why shopping malls and department-store escalators are set up the way they are. If you are forced to pass all those other stores and all that extra merchandise, you are much more likely to purchase something on top of what you went there to buy. Do not let this logic apply to you. Look but don't pay!

• **Off the beaten track.** There are a million nooks and crannies where a bargain can be hidden. Spelunk! Explore the places you would not ordinarily shop. Check the phone book, garage sales, charity events, church bazaars, thrift shops, flea markets, even salvage stores and the Salvation Army. When you carry your pride within yourself, there is no need to be concerned about any stigma attached to these places. Rich people certainly aren't!

In fact, wealthy people tend to donate their things to places such as these, and savvy bargain hunters know and take advantage of this. Antiques, collectibles, luxurious clothing and furniture (perhaps in slight need of repair) all can be found second-hand for a fraction of their original cost.

• **Realize that you are paying for a brand's name popularity.** While there are a few brand names that are indisputably equated with high quality (types of automobiles and stereos), in most cases one can of corn niblets is truly no better or worse than the next. People who pay extra to buy a product because it is a popular brand name may well be losing out in the long run. That extra money you've spent is actually going toward bigger advertising, snazzier packaging, and corporate think tanks employed to come up with ways to keep that brand name in the public eye! Drop your preconceptions, do a little research, and check out less expensive brands. If the difference is minimal, switch.

Beware the Coupon Myth

We have all heard about the woman who collected, clipped, and assembled her coupons so diligently that she saved over $150 on a single trip to the supermarket, walking away with a cartload of products virtually free. There are two elements of this story, however, that are not heard about as frequently.

1. This woman did not have a life! Her so-called hobby of coupon-clipping was really the equivalent of a full-time job, where between ten and thirty hours a week were devoted to scouring publications, snipping her way through papers, filing, and mailing away for premiums to get more coupons. If we were to look at wages conservatively, say about $6 an hour, this woman spent about $180 worth of time and effort to pull off her one-shot $150 shopping spree.

2. This woman adjusted her shopping habits to accommodate the coupons! She pursued products she really didn't need and would never have ordinarily purchased because some of her coupons offered such "big savings." Actually, she wound up "spending" more. While this is not so evident in her miracle shopping spree, it will stare her in the face when she does her regular shopping. She is allowing the glamour of big savings to set an agenda for her, warp her shopping list to include clutter, and dictate what she buys. In the end, she'll be lucky if she breaks even!

Big business is insidious. If coupons really cut down on how much you pay at the cash register, corporations would be losing money instead of making more! Coupons are devices to get you to buy something new, something more, or something you would not ordinarily have considered trying. Coupons and sales premiums such as stamps, mail-ins, contests, and the like are fine, so long as they serve your purposes and discount the purchases you planned to make. Otherwise, they are useless. Beware of them!

Buying Generic

Manufacturers who regularly find themselves with a surplus of a product will often liquidate their overflow by repackaging and reselling this surplus to supermarket chains and discount outlets. Frozen foods, pet foods, beverages, cereals, and paper products are among the dozens of consumables offered at cut rates, and the stores take advantage of these extremely low wholesale prices by offering "no frills," generic, or in-store brand products to their customers. Of course, the names have to be changed to protect the guilty, but by this logic why not share in the savings? Shrug off the snootiness and switch over!

It is true, not all generic products will meet with your satisfaction. But it is important to determine whether this is because of some defect in the product itself or because you have some built-in bias against white boxes! The supermarket chains keep prices on no-frills items low by not spending any more than they have to on package design, coloring, snappy names, or nifty advertising gimmicks. Test out the generic equivalents of your deodorant, aspirin, toothpaste, vitamins, paper cups, and so forth. Savings of 20 percent, 30 percent, and even 60 percent, when held against comparable name-brand products, should provide an incentive. And if you really can't stand the packaging, take the product home and empty it into some of those wonderful plastic storage containers you bought after reading Chapter 3.

Incidentally, supermarkets and discount outlets are not the only places you will find "generic" products. No-frills versions of vitamin supplements, cereals (pennies for a pound of healthy rolled oats vs. $2.99 for an eleven-ounce box of processed Cheerios!), herbs, spices, and other items of interest can be found in your neighborhood health food store. Rural general stores and waterside fish and produce markets offer this same type of fantastic bargain potential.

Discount Outlets

Just as supermarkets acquire generic products, discount

outlets receive manufacturers' overstock originally meant for hardware stores, department stores, specialty shops, and so forth. For the same reasons that generic product packaging is bland, these places are not usually attractive to look at. Also, prices may vary from outlet to outlet, week to week, so don't purchase blindly. Find the ones in your area and get on their mailing lists. Some of the larger discount chains have developed membership programs. They distribute cards that can bring you even greater savings. Remember, you'll only be able to bank the cash if you stick to the reason you left the house in the first place.

Buying in Bulk

Society is accustomed to weekly foraging. We take our paychecks and hit the shopping centers for weekly sales. But if you open your mind to alternatives, you can break that seven-day cycle and save a bundle. Warehouse, salvage, and liquidation stores as well as food co-ops are all capable of slashing per-capita prices on name-brand products by selling them to you in bulk.

Now rid yourself of those images of hillbillies and their families loading up their flatbeds with six bushels of apples and the back half of a frozen steer! While your initial investment may seem a bit high, keep in mind that purchasing products in bulk will give you a several week supply. When it all evens out, you can save over $50 in grocery bills for that first month's purchase and substantially more as you continue.

There are huge depots and just-above-wholesale outlets currently opening all over the country. Many of them are more than simply farmers' markets. Housewares, sporting, and gardening equipment, even lumber, construction equipment, and cars are sold alongside canned foods and produce at sizeable discounts. As with anything recommended here, compare prices (keep a record of them) and plot your course. You may want to hit more than one on a trip.

You can find wholesale distributors in the *Yellow Pages*, possibly in the category of your particular needs and interests. Some of the larger bakeries distribute to smaller cake shops, but may sell a dozen freezable loaves to you for pennies a piece! A beverage distributor might be found under "Restaurant Supplies," for example. Give them a call first: Some distributors don't sell directly to individuals or may have a minimum order. If this is the case, ask for leads. Tell them you'll let the store or co-op know who sent you.

If you still can't find a good source of products sold in bulk, send a self-addressed stamped envelope to: Co-op Directory Services, 919 21st Ave. S., Minneapolis, Minnesota 55404. They'll send you names of regional wholesalers, who in turn can provide you with the names and addresses of local buying clubs, co-ops, and discount outlets. Do a little research, make room for a little extra in your cabinets, attic, or closets, and hack away at those shopping bills!

Government Auctions

When law enforcement agents confiscate property, or products and merchandise fall into the hands of the government in one form or another, auctions are held to liquidate the inventory. While quality and variety can run the full spectrum, the remarkable savings potential makes these auctions worth looking into. It is not unheard of for contemporary models of mechanically sound cars to sell for $500 or less. Desirable real estate can be gotten for a song. Contact the following sources to find out more about local government auctions and real estate programs:

US Department of Housing and Urban Development
451 7th St. SW
Washington, D.C. 20410-4000

Qualified buyers can purchase homes through HUD at fractions of their original cost. You can move into some of them with no more than a $100 down payment, with mortgage payments of no more than 29 percent of your monthly gross income. These homes have been acquired by the department because of foreclosures caused by political or economic conditions, or because the property was seized during criminal prosecution. Neighborhoods vary but can often be quite pleasant. To find the Department of Housing and Urban Development regional office nearest you, call 202-708-1422. For *A Home of Your Own*, a step-by-step guide to buying HUD property, call the HUD Homeline at 800-767-4483. For other money-saving HUD programs that may interest you, call 202-708-0685.

US Customs Service
E.G.& G Dynatrend
2300 Clarendon Blvd., Suite 705
Arlington, Virginia 22201

Auctions on forfeited and confiscated general merchandise, including vehicles, machinery, clothing, jewelry, household goods, furniture, liquor, and high-tech equipment, are held across the country. These items are sold by lot, and you must make your decisions carefully, but savings can be remarkable. For more information, call the US Customs Public Auction Line at 703-351-7887. They can tell you where and when the next auction will be held in your area. You can also request a subscription to a list of detailed descriptions of items up for sale, either nationwide ($50 per year) or by region ($25 per year).

Wholesale by Mail

The showstopper of all bargain sources has to be shopping wholesale by mail or over the telephone. You would be amazed at how many corporations and manufacturers will forego the middle man and sell their product directly to you at wholesale prices, which can run anywhere from 30 percent to 90 percent off what you'd see on the retail tag.

What are the catches? There aren't many and most of them are minor:

- You'll probably need a credit card, though if you're willing to wait a bit longer for your purchase, cashier's checks and money orders are perfectly acceptable.
- You'll have to employ a little of that patience we talked about. This is not shopping by impulse or for instant gratification. Delivery, however, is usually fast and can often be arranged around your schedule.
- Many wholesale sources will have minimum orders or a set amount you have to spend before they will sell to you, but these can both be much lower than you might think.
- You simply must not be tempted to buy more than you absolutely need just because the prices on everything are like a stroll through the Pearly Gates!

The best way to determine whether an item you are interested in is sold wholesale directly from the manufacturer is to find out who makes the product, locate their 800 number in that nifty AT&T directory we discussed, and ask. Customer service departments should be equipped to handle just such questions.

Here are just a few examples of companies that sell their products direct to consumers at wholesale prices:

No Nonsense Direct
P.O. Box 26095
Greensboro, North Carolina 27420-6095
Sells pantyhose directly to you for 50 percent off retail price. Send for a free brochure.

Sportswear Clearinghouse
P.O. Box 317746
Cincinnati, Ohio 45231-7746
Sells basic (nothing in "neon" colors) sports apparel and accessories for up to a whopping 70 percent off retail. Send for a free brochure.

The Ultimate Outlet
P.O. Box 88251
Chicago, Illinois 60680-1251
A vast array of products. Whatever it is, they can reliably get it for you wholesale! Some of the savings can run as high as 70 percent! Send $2 for a catalog.

Betty Crocker Enterprises
P.O. Box 5348
Minneapolis, Minnesota 55460
It ain't just cakes! Kitchen ware, housewares, even toys for up to 77 percent off retail. Send 50¢ for a catalog.

Beautiful Visions USA
810 S Broadway, Suite 299
Hicksville, New York 11801
A reliable source for virtually any name brand cosmetic or toiletry. There are reasonable ways to save up to a pulse-pounding 90 percent off on these expensive items. Send $1 for a catalog.

Quill Corporation
100 Schelter Rd.
Lincolnshire, Illinois 60197-4700

One of the great standards for office supplies and equipment. Savings can reach 70 percent off retail. Be sure to send your request for a free catalog on business letterhead.

Where do the rich get their furniture? Well, where we all get it, North Carolina, of course! Except we go to our local department stores for that superb North Carolina furniture, while the wealthy know that the secret to quality furnishings at extremely low prices is to go straight to the manufacturer. The following is a brief list of home and office furniture, carpeting, and drapery manufacturers from whom you may purchase directly at an average savings of 50 percent off retail:

Barnes & Barnes Furniture
190 Commerce Avenue
Southern Pines, North Carolina 28387
Phone: 800-334-8174

Save up to 55 percent on home furnishings with a 50 percent deposit. Call for their free brochure.

Cherry Hill Furniture, Carpet & Interiors
P.O. Box 7405
Furniture Land Station
High Point, North Carolina 27264
Phone: 800-888-0933

Home and office furniture, draperies, and accessories at savings of up to 50 percent. Call with inquiries and for their free brochure.

Liberty Green
P.O. Box 5035

Wilmington, North Carolina 28403
Phone: 800-255-9704

Save up to 60 percent on country-style furnishings for
your home. Send $3 for a catalog, refundable with your
first purchase. Satisfaction guaranteed.

Loftin-Black
111 Sedgehill Dr.
Thomasville, North Carolina 27360
Phone: 800-334-7398

Specializing in bedding and accessories, save up to 50
percent off. Ask about in-home delivery and set up, as
well as free brochure.

Plexi-Craft Quality Products
514 W 24th Street
New York, New York 10011-1179

Though this company is based in New York City, it is one
of the best for mail-order bathroom fixtures and various
types of accessory tables. Send $2 for their catalog.

6 | *Barter: The Oldest Form of Commerce*

You Scratch My Back

Before there was such a thing as currency, buying and selling between people consisted of swapping the things they had for the things they needed. If you needed a bushel of wheat for this month's hotcakes, then you found someone who had it and traded that leg of woolly mammoth that had been lying around gathering flies in the cave. Trade agreements were made in direct response to mutual need, and not a greenback or gold bar entered in the picture. Wouldn't it be a help to revive such a tradition? Instead of paying someone to scratch your back, it would be a simple matter of tickling that person's toes in return

As with any business transaction, the secret of barter lies in your ability to assess both what someone has to offer and what that person needs. If an individual you meet has a skill or business that can be of use to you, whether right now or some time in the future, make note of it. Then listen! Keep your ears open for what this person might need. You don't have to have it right now, be it skill or possession, to make a barter work sometime down the road. Perhaps you know someone who can be of service to this person. Maybe one day you will have something that can be of use to your potential barter mate.

Once you do have something to offer, the key to a good

barter is offering it first! By acknowledging your potential barter partner's needs and making an initial offer, you are establishing a friendly environment in which to deal. As your offer is considered, you can reinforce your position by indicating that you have no intention of charging money for your service. You need not even ask for something in return right away. This will please the person you are dealing with. Your service will be remembered, and the favor most likely returned. Exchanging services, skills, and items you have in abundance for the things you need can save you thousands of dollars a year!

Assessing What You've Got

Sit down and make a list of the things you have to offer: specialties, areas of expertise, skills in which you have some degree of confidence. Can you sew? Write? Do taxes? Balance books? Babysit? Tutor? Do you have leeway with your business to provide a little free service on the side? Can you organize? Cater? Tend bar? Raise funds? Do you have a craft or artistic skills? What are you best at, and how can this help people? Do you have a collection you could part with? Overstock gathering dust? Get a friend or partner to help you if you must, but write it all down, everything you have to contribute. Remember to keep things within the realm of feasibility. What you are prepared to do should not cost so much time and effort as not to be worth whatever it is you'd be getting in return!

Then take into account all the areas of expertise, business acumen, skills, services, and abilities many of your friends and relatives can supply. One of the secrets to successful barter is being able to put people who can benefit one another in contact. This establishes a network that will ultimately benefit you. Close-knit associations of well-to-do people like the Kiwanis Club, the Lions Club, and Freemasons are perfect examples of successful barter networks. Make a name for yourself helping people to get what they want for no cash payment, and it will be that much easier to start asking for the things you need free of charge.

Establishing a System of Contacts

All too often people enter into social situations with strangers and remain aloof. You stick with the people you know at that cocktail party, leaving the "strangers" to talk among themselves. Next time you are in such a situation, however, look at things this way: Each of those "strangers" is a potential bartering partner. It's often hard to tell what people do based solely on their appearance. You'd be surprised!

As an exercise, in the next situation where you find yourself with people you don't know really well, seek out someone and steer the conversation toward what the person does, what the person's interests are, and what the person needs or can use to make life a little easier. If a match has been made, go for it! Get that person's business card or phone number. If you know someone who might be able to help, put the two in touch. They will both thank you for it. When you go home, make a note of this person, what he does, and how to contact him or her. This type of networking will only get easier as you keep doing it!

The Rolodex

It has often been said, the bigger the Rolodex, the wealthier the person who owns it. Whether for barter or for any number of other excellent reasons, go out and purchase a large wheellike Rolodex (or pocket-size computer if you're feeling ritzy and can get one at a discount), and start filling it up! Everyone you know has the potential to do some kind of business, and business can be bartered for something you can offer. Take those notes and business cards you've been collecting during the exercises we've discussed and transfer them onto your Rolodex. Include appropriate notes.

A thousand names will do you no good if you don't use them. Establish that network and stay connected. Keep track of who you've put together with whom. Stay in touch without being a pest. Review the section in this book about handling telephone calls and remember to keep things short and sweet. People may want you to believe they have all the time in the world, but they really don't, especially if they are wealthy.

Pooling Your Resources

Barter can also be subtle, even symbiotic, and you've probably seen examples of it every day. The general exchange of food or clothing between friends and neighbors, car-pooling in order to get to work, or coffee-pooling once you all get there. Consider the following low-cost or no-cost possibilities by pooling your resources as well as those of your friends and coworkers, and your mate and relatives:

- **Entertain at home.** Pull some compatible people out of that Rolodex and start taking turns with modest dinner parties, sports gatherings, TV/video nights, or music listening sit-ins at home. Prepare food and amusement cheaply. Don't order out; cook at home. Follow frugal recipes and be sure that everyone can eat what you prepare.
- **Start a lunch club.** If you are already preparing your lunches at home, it might not take much additional effort to make a little extra to bring in one day a week to share with coworkers. Making more of the same is much less expensive than

preparing five different meals. A lunch club with
three or four coworkers can be fun and cut costs
dramatically.

- **Bring a few people together to buy in bulk or
  meet wholesale minimums.** If you find you need
  something, but don't need that much of it or can't
  afford minimum costs or quantities, bring a record
  of the price or brochure or catalog to a few
  acquaintances and offer them the opportunity to
  get in on a bargain. Let them know when you're
  looking for the same item.
- **Circulate things you would ordinarily throw out
  or put away.** Activate your books, magazines, trade
  publications, music or video tapes, computer
  programs, clothing accessories, and other items by
  circulating them among your coworkers or friends
  and have them do the same with their items. If
  something comes along that you'd really like to
  keep, barter for it when the circuit is finished.

Part II
Living Wealthy
on the System

7 | *Knowledge Is Wealth*

Information Can Save You Big Money

As the information age washes around us, it is vital for you to realize that wealth is born of knowledge. Figuring out how to access data which can help you in your quest to accumulate wealth is three-quarters of the battle. For those of us who were not raised with computers in our classrooms, or digital fiber optics in our phone lines, the forthcoming information super highway may seem daunting. But those of us who refuse to be intimidated by this data explosion can learn to harness its power and use it to increase our wealth.

Look It Up

The first step in making information save and earn you big money is to admit to yourself that you don't know something when in fact you don't. Keeping yourself in the dark will only prove to be a disservice to you. So much of what keeps us poor is the lack of not simply "schooling," but *education*. Like a starving person in the desert who trudges within a hundred yards of a village, but does not see it because he has no map, the knowledge you need to become truly successful could be somewhere in your own home!

When you gather knowledge, you are making yourself wiser and more articulate. When you smoothly incorporate your knowledge into conversation, you become impressive and respected. Wealthy people recognize people who seem to know what they are talking about and give them jobs. When you have thoroughly investigated a certain field, you can discuss it with confidence.

Pursue your interests with vigor. Take a casual or superficial knowledge of something and turn it into a specialty. Shine a light into those dark areas just beyond your field of perception. If you are not as rich as you would like to be right now, the answers may very well exist somewhere close by.

This does not have to be a painful or costly exercise. Here are some common and inexpensive ways to become brilliant:

Reference books. Use your household dictionary, thesaurus, encyclopedia, almanac, atlas, and phone book to get the facts about your subject.

Magazines and trade publications. So many of us are taken up with the glamour of various occupations and lifestyles. Specialty magazines and publications created specifically for people in certain occupations can shed new light on subjects you're only acquainted with through TV or superficial periodicals.

Specialty publications (such as *Variety* or the *Hollywood Reporter*, if movies intrigue you, for example) can teach you the "language" of your area of interest—the vocabulary and phraseology that can give you access to certain circles or cliques within a profession.

The library. Whether it is your neighborhood public library or collections at your area hospital, university, or technical school, these places continue to offer the cheapest, easiest ways to gather solid information. Often forgotten are the periodical sections, which can contain cutting-edge information in the form of articles in trade and collegiate publications. And don't be afraid to ask for help! That is why there are librarians on staff. Also, many libraries have services that can answer questions about virtually anything over the telephone. Look into this!

Audit classes and seminars. There is nothing to stop you from attending courses that might interest you at local colleges and universities without having to pay for them. You might make a direct request of the professor to audit a few classes or simply take an empty seat in one of the larger auditoriums and take notes.

Keep up with what is happening on your local campus. Seminars, film and arts programs, cultural activities, and all kinds of other events occur at colleges on a daily basis— and they are often free and open to the public. Consult listings in your local newspapers for off-campus forums and seminars of interest at places like town halls, museums, and libraries. Put passion into your pursuit!

On-line access. Purchase a modem for your computer, hook it into your telephone line, and subscribe to an inexpensive on-line service, such as Prodigy or Compuserve. Nowhere else is there such lively discussion and discourse from such a wide variety of participants. Many say on-line communication and data exchange will become as commonplace as picking up your telephone.

Consult with an expert. People love to share their interests, and they appreciate a good listening ear. Find someone you can be certain knows a lot about what it is you need to know, then ask questions. Treat this person with respect and you will have a valuable source of experience and information. For more on the subject of experts, turn to Chapter 11.

Hard knowledge can turn into deep understanding and even wisdom when it is shared. Talk about what you've learned with people whose intelligence you respect. Encourage questions, so that you can apply what you've learned in a conversational context. All that information will do you no good if you can't communicate it clearly in a way that the layman can understand.

Wrangling the System

With patience, persistence, and politeness, ways can be found to solve most problems and cut down expenses in any situation. A fabulous network of support exists along the back roads and side streets of this data expressway, and by using some of the hints and leads in this book, virtually any kind of assistance can be requested free of charge!

The chapters that comprise Part Two of this book should not be construed as definitive. Consider them examples of places to easily obtain information where most people might not think to look. Our government, for instance, has so often been portrayed as bumbling and incompetent, or prying and menacing, that few people realize it has thousands of departments and suborganizations meant only to help us. Only a mere sampling follows in subsequent chapters, but you should get the picture. The same can be said for consumer relations departments in large corporations, public relations offices in colleges and universities, and assistance programs at libraries and museums.

Human beings have an innate desire to please one another, so long as they feel appreciated for doing so. By acknowledging the contributions of others with thanks, or some small gift or act of kindness in return, you are creating a doorway through which you can enter time and again.

Establish your agenda, then forget about any fears you might have about logically following it to a conclusion. Remember, you have a vision that you are pursuing as if your life depended on it. You mustn't be put off by being placed on hold or told to go somewhere else to find what you need. Move through the system rapidly, with a clear notion of your goals, and the system will work to make you wealthy.

8 | *Travel*

Plotting Your Course

With the economy currently as tight as it is, the travel industry has taken a beating. Belt-tightening has eliminated many airplane trips, hotel stays, and vacations abroad. The industry itself has responded by attempting to lure you away from your home with premiums, packages, and promotions that can sometimes sound too good to be true. Well, some of them are and some of them aren't. The trick is to plot your course carefully by breaking down each and every offer, demanding the most for your money and making certain you're getting exactly what you want.

Whether you are traveling by plane, cruise ship, or railroad, and whether your stay is at a country inn or luxury hotel, you must remember that you are spending money to be well accommodated. Within reason, the travel industry is there to serve you, and there is no reason why you should expect to be treated as anything less than a well-respected client. If the so-called minor or detail services are not immediately apparent when you consult with an agent or hotel about an aspect of your trip, ask for them! Here are some examples of services you might not be aware of that are often available during travel. Any combination of them can ring up some remarkable savings.

Accumulate air miles. Virtually every major airline offers frequent-flyer service through which you can accumulate hundreds and thousands of "air miles" every time you fly with a given company. When you have accumulated a certain preset number of miles, the airline will offer you tremendous discounts on future trips or even free tickets to any number of destinations worldwide. When combined with air clubs, credit card "air-mileage" promotions, and discount travel agency usage, you can literally earn free airplane tickets within months. A little strategic planning and you can eventually journey to locales around the world for next to nothing! Remember, this does not work unless you ask for your frequent-flyer application the next time you travel and remain loyal to a particular airline. Learn the procedure for accumulating those miles and don't forget to do so whenever you fly.

Join travel clubs and learn about your destination's Traveler's Aid Society. Check your local newspapers and regional magazines for listings on travel clubs and explorer's organizations. Together, these clubs can book discount air fares, group rates, cruises, and tours at big savings. Many air and cruise lines offer their own travel clubs, which you may join free of charge. Services offered by these clubs include substantial discounts on tickets, cut rates at hotels and restaurants around the world, and even personal insurance policies. Contact your favorite carrier's customer service department for details. If you truly love to travel and do so often you may want to subscribe to *Travel Smart* ($37; 40 Beechdale Road, Dobbs Ferry, New York 10522-9989), an excellent newsletter that offers extensive information on hotel, airfare, cruise and car rental bargains, as well as discount travel opportunities of all kinds.

Also, your destination area's Tourist Board or Traveler's Aid Society is committed to making your stay as comfortable and interesting as possible. Contact them via their 800 number and get the goods on as many free and low-cost services as they can offer!

Take advantage of educational travel offers. Many colleges also open student cultural/education vacations to nonstudent tourists who are interested in widening their horizons. You can save thousands of dollars using student discounts throughout your trip. Contact your local college adult or continuing education department for details. And if you don't mind roughing it a bit, check out the *Travel Accommodations Guide,* which details ways in which you can stay on campus at universities around the world for as low as $19 per night as well as offering dozens of other money-saving tips. Send $13 to Campus Travel Service, P.O. Box 5007, Laguna Beach, California 92652.

Demand to be pampered! Most of us only get a week or two off each year to vacation and relax. You are perfectly within your rights to ask for anything that you may need to have a wonderful time, and, believe it or not, people in the travel industry want your business and are prepared to give it to you! Ask for free breakfast service (many hotels offer this, but you have to ask!), extra pillows, free tours, discount theater tickets, access to local cultural festivals, free transport to and from your hotel.

If you are not getting what you want, threaten to go somewhere else. It's best, of course, to plot these demands at home and bring them to the bargaining table *before* you start your trip, but don't let that stop you if it's already under way. Reward your drivers, bellhops, and concierges with solid tips for good, money-saving recommendations. Take names and hint that you will write letters if service is unsatisfactory. A company called Travelbooks, 113 Corporation Road, Hyannis, Massachusetts 02601-2204, offers a wide variety of publications about matters such as these. Call 800-869-3535 for their catalog.

Saving on Wheels

Whether you're driving to work on a daily basis, taking a spin over to the next town, or preparing a cross-country trip, there are several things you can do to get the best buy possible on auto purchases and secure your car so that you can be assured lowest possible costs in case of emergency.

Here are a few information sources to help you save thousands on car purchases, as well as emergency services:

Consumer Reports
Box 8005
Novi, Michigan 48376

In addition to publishing an excellent magazine, this organization offers the superb *Consumer Reports Auto Price Service*, which provides information on negotiating the lowest possible price for the auto of your choice. Write them for more information, and enclose a self-addressed stamped envelope for fastest service.

Better Business Bureau
4200 Wilson Blvd., Suite 800
Arlington, Virginia 22203

The BBB provides guides to buying cars, tires, and other merchandise at low rates. Send your request for information with a business-size, self-addressed stamped envelope to their Publications Department.

American Automobile Association (AAA)
Call 800-336-4357 for the chapter nearest you. Although there are a number of excellent travel clubs, AAA's rates have actually gone down in recent years, while services have increased! In addition to emergency towing, the organization offers extensive travel planning, including free maps and travel books, car rental discounts, no-fee traveler's checks, special services for international trips,

personal accident insurance, and other benefits (which do
vary from chapter to chapter).

Take on a Few Travel Agents

When you think about it, why should a travel agent bring
you the lowest rates humanly possible? These people work
on commission and business can be slow. How much can
they make if you launch yourself from New York to L.A. for
$99, even if such a fare were available? It pays to take on
three or four travel agents (from separate agencies, not
separate branches of the same agency) and compare prices.
If an agent is truly worth the golden money you're parting
with, that person will have access to a variety of sources of
travel information.

Discount travel agents are aptly named. They make up for
small commissions on truly low rates by acquiring a
multitude of clients and developing a solid reputation for
quality.

Farefinders, 11899 West Pico Blvd., West Los Angeles,
California 90064 (213-479-6313), is one such discount
agency. Cruises Worldwide, 16585 Von Karman, Irvine,
California 92714, is Farefinders' ocean-going counterpart,
offering discounts of up to 50 percent on advertised rates.
Call 800-6-CRUISE for more information.

Again, whenever traveling be certain that what you are
getting suits your agenda, and not someone else's. There are
always other places from which to purchase tickets, so you
can afford to be demanding. Read all the fine print, go into
cancellation policies, and always know whom to contact at
every point in your trip.

Bucket Seating

One way wealthy people pull huge savings out of travel is
to establish direct lines to consolidators. Often referred to in

the travel industry as "bucket shops," consolidators purchase blocks of airplane seats from airlines and resell them for far less than the going rate. Travel agents turn good profits by purchasing these tickets from bucket shops and dumping you in them. Your savings can start at 25 percent off advertised rates, and skyrocket from there (especially if you are flying economy), depending on where you want to go and how soon you need to get there. Consolidators can also offer bookings on cruise ships, hotel rooms, and chartered transport.

Two examples of reliable bucket shops are the Unitravel Corporation (800-325-2222) and Council Charter (800-223-7402). Both sell to individuals and book national and international flights. Contact them at least a month before you plan to travel. Occasionally, seats won't turn up until shortly before your date of departure. Be absolutely clear when making all travel arrangements and get confirmations in writing whenever possible. It can also help to try and track down travel brokers (as opposed to agents) in your area.

Cutting Hotel and Restaurant Costs

There can be no substitute for research and planning when you travel, even if what you seek is adventure and spontaneity. No one wants the disaster of mismanaged travel arrangements, misunderstood instructions, or lousy dining experiences. Consult with people who have been to a place before you and listen to their recommendations. Avoid tourist traps by picking up on local media and going where the natives enjoy themselves.

Travel America at HalfPrice ($32.95) and *HalfPrice Europe* ($70), both from Entertainment Publications, 2125 Butterfield Rd., Troy, Michigan 48084 (800-477-3234), offer fantastic savings on food and lodging. Each directory comes with a membership card and coupons which apply to over 1,200 hotels and motels and 1,300 restaurants (at 25 percent discounts) across the country. These deals are simply amazing if you travel at all; other books are available for specific locales.

9 | *Health*

Secrets to Low-Cost Medicine

The cost of health maintenance and treatment will always wind up being the most expensive item of anyone's budget. The health industry, including diet, exercise, apparel, equipment, medical, pharmaceutical, optical, and a myriad other subindustries makes billions by taking advantage of ailing consumers. Any opportunity to safely undercut the health industry giants is to be encouraged. Prevention, of course, is your best bet. Strengthen yourself and live healthy rather than pay the price of treating symptoms. Surgery must be seen as a last resort, as costs spiral into the stratosphere at this point. Opt for nonsurgical procedures whenever possible

Setting aside time and space to exercise at home (perhaps with a series of inexpensive videotapes or recorded cable TV exercise programs) can save you hundreds on gym fees; joining community exercise programs can do the same. Put yourself on mailing lists of local nonprofit organizations such as the Lung Association. They often send out special offers for joining gyms and health clubs free of charge. Free, thorough physicals are often offered at teaching or university affiliated hospitals, where professional physicians oversee examinations conducted by interns and residents.

If at this point you cannot afford health insurance, or

your small business is unable to provide it for you, there is an interesting legal loophole you can leap through to receive free medical care. Under the National Hill-Burton law, if you meet certain income requirements there should be no charge to you for care at hospitals and other health-care facilities which receive federal funding for construction and modernization. Call the Department of Health and Human Services at 800-638-0742 for more information.

A relatively little known way to attain low-cost medication is through the mail. There are several pharmaceutical companies which offer discounts of up to 60 percent off what you would pay filling your prescriptions at the drug store. While these include generic versions of popular medications (which are perfectly fine substitutes), they also carry a wide variety of name brands. Keep in mind that, when it comes to medicine, not everything is discounted. Compare prices before using these services. Fast delivery can be arranged in an emergency, and these companies take checks, money orders, and credit cards. What follow are the names and addresses of a few reliable discount pharmaceutical companies:

Family Pharmaceuticals of America
P.O. Box 1288
Mount Pleasant, South Carolina 29465-1288
Phone 800-922-3444

They can quote prices by phone and you can save up to 60 percent on prescription drugs. They tend to concentrate on fulfilling orders made by people with serious illnesses such as cancer, organ transplants, and AIDS. Their invoices are designed to ease reimbursement from insurance companies. Their price list is free of charge.

Medi-Mail
P.O. Box 98520

Las Vegas, Nevada 89193-8520
Phone 800-331-1458

While discounts may not be as steep here, the staff is
friendly and informative, and the prices are competitive.
An additional 20 percent discount is offered on generic
drugs. They will also give price quotes over the phone
and offer health-care and beauty aids as well. Their
brochure is free.

Pharmail Corporation
P.O. Box 1466
Champlain, New York 12919-1466
Phone 800-237-8927

You can save on an average of 50 percent on name-brand
and generic drugs with this prescription fulfillment
service. And savings rise dramatically after that, if your
needs require supplies over the course of months. They
also offer health-care products and vitamins. Minimum
order is $25; call or send a SASE for more information.

Skin Deep Without Empty Pockets

Cosmetics, vitamins, and toiletries can by among the
most expensive items of daily life. What major department
stores charge for health and beauty aids can be simply
shocking, and yet many of us choose to accept these
exorbitant prices as a fact of life. Needless to say, we don't
have to.

As with most other products, when you buy perfume,
makeup, dietary supplements, or hair-care treatments, you
are paying as much for the fancy venue (and the even fancier
salesclerk) as you are for the item. The range in price
between Macy's and your local discount drug store for the
same brand of lipstick can be vast! Buying an identical
product in a ritzier store *simply does not make the product
better!*

With this in mind, the following is a brief list of places from which you can order name-brand cosmetics (Max Factor, L'Oreal, Sassoon, and Revlon, to name a few), skincare products, toiletries, and dietary supplements, even exercise equipment, jewelry, and gifts, at up to a staggering 90 percent off:

Hillstad International
1545 Berger Dr.
San Jose, California 95112
Phone: 800-535-7742

Vitamins, dietary supplements, toiletries, and soaps for up to 40 percent off. Send for their free catalog.

Kettle Care
1535 Eagle Dr.
Kalispell, Montana 59901

Specializing in all-natural bath and skin-care products at an average savings of 30 percent. Send $1 for their catalog.

Creative Health Products
5148 Saddle Ridge Road
Plymouth, Missouri 48170
Phone 800-742-4478

Name-brand exercise equipment, some of which is quite expensive, at discounts of around 30 percent. Send for their free catalog.

Beautiful Visions USA
810 S Broadway, Suite 299
Hicksville, New York 11801

Satisfaction is guaranteed on virtually any brand name makeups, toiletries, hair-care products, jewelry, and gifts. Savings up to 90 percent of retail price. Send $1 for their catalog.

The Eyes Have It

There is never a reason to pay full price for corrective lenses, whether eyeglasses or contacts. Wait for promotions at the larger chains, two for the price of one, and so forth. Do not rely completely on examinations at eyeglass stores and certainly do not consider them replacements for yearly visits to your eye doctor. Eyewear store exams should be given free of charge, and you should be entitled to know what your prescription is when you're done. Do not settle for less.

As with furniture and other products, it pays a lot to go to the source when it comes to glasses and contacts. You can save up to 50 percent off retail prices on both lenses and frames, so long as you know your exact prescription. Here are a few services you can contact for major discounts on eyewear:

Prism Optical
10992 NW 77th Ave.
North Miami, Florida 33168
They offer a variety of eyeglass lens types and a fair selection of designer frames at 30 percent to 50 percent off what you would pay at an eyeglass store. Their catalog costs $2, which is refundable on your first purchase.

National Contact Lens Center
3527 Bonita Vista Dr.
Santa Rosa, California 95404-1506
An extremely reliable way of getting name-brand hard or soft contact lenses, with savings rising as high as a soul-stirring 75 percent! Remember, they cannot fit you with lenses or provide first-timer services. Their brochure is free and they can give you a quote if you send them a SASE.

Elite Eyewear
P.O. Box 680030

North Miami, Florida 33168

They offer up to 50 percent off designer eyeglass frames
and sunglasses. You can fit the lenses you get at your
local eyeglass store with the frames you receive from
Elite. Their brochure is free when you write to them.

Seek Out Doctors' Coalitions

While the establishment of a viable national health-care
program is still years away, there are some interesting
developments on a more regional level for those who seek
low-cost medical treatment. General practitioners,
podiatrists, chiropractors, and even dentists have been
forming local coalitions and offering discounts on
consultation and treatment to subscribers to their services.
These doctors pool their resources and advertise as a group,
wherein a single annual fee will get you a list of
participating physicians and discounts of up to 50 percent
off treatment. Prices vary, of course, but your own doctor or
dentist may be connected with one of these groups, without
your even knowing it! Ask!

The name and number of your local coalition may be
listed in your regional *Yellow Pages* under the health
concern that interests you, or you can go to your
neighborhood library and enlist the assistance of a friendly
librarian.

AARP is Not Just for the Elderly

You don't have to be 65 to join one of the most beneficial
and cost-cutting organizations in the nation. The American
Association of Retired Persons is a tremendous non-profit
organization devoted to improving the standard of living for
any American fifty years or older. The emphasis in their
work is on health issues and finance, both pertinent to this
discussion.

At a cost of $5 per year you can receive their magazine, *Modern Maturity,* and monthly bulletins, the opportunity to purchase low-cost supplemental health, auto, and homeowner's insurance, publications on health issues, discounts for travel-related services, and the keys to their mail-order prescription and over-the-counter drug service. Write to the American Association of Retired Persons (AARP), 601 E St. NW, Washington, D.C. 20049 for more information. Also, request their free *Prescription for Action* publication on health-care issues and money-saving recommendations.

10 | *Income Tax*

Filing for Nothing

Though it may seem unlikely at first, and if you've got nothing to hide, why pay money to expensive tax preparers, tax accountants, and tax attorneys when you can get most of what they offer—only better—and at no cost to you? The government has a variety of free programs very few people know about. Contact the District Offices of the Internal Revenue Service at 800-829-1040 for a complete list of these services, which include:

IRS Tax Computation
District Offices
Internal Revenue Service
US Department of the Treasury
1111 Constitution Ave., NW, Room 2704
Washington, D.C. 20224
Phone 800-829-1040

If you use Form 1040A, the IRS will complete the calculations for your taxes. Simply fill in the tax return through Line 20. All income must be from wages and interest. There are other minor stipulations, so contact the above number for more information.

Electronic Tax Filing Division
Internal Revenue Service

1111 Constitution Ave.,
Washington, D.C. 20224
Phone 202-535-9725

Electronic filing of tax returns is faster and easier because
there is less work involved in the reviewing process.
Savings are found in doing the computer work yourself
(help is available at the above number), in postage, and in
the fact that you will get your refund check faster than
any returns received by conventional means. Contact this
office to see if you qualify.

Forms, Education, and Legal Aid—All Free

Any tax forms you could possibly need should be
available at your local library, post office, or technical
school. If they are not, place a request for a specific form you
need with the person in charge there. Forms may be ordered
by these facilities by contacting the Taxpayer Service
Division of the Internal Revenue Service at 202-566-6352.
You can order tax forms directly from the IRS by calling
800-424-3676. Libraries also will often have audio or video
cassettes which provide detailed instructions on how to file
your taxes.

Free courses in how to prepare taxes for yourself, as well
as free assistance in preparing your taxes, are available in
cities across the country. These courses are staffed by law
school and graduate accounting students, who are
supervised by their professors. For a list of locations nearest
you, call 202-566-6352. If you want to speak directly with
IRS staff consultants on any aspect of filling out your forms,
call 800-829-1040 or contact your local IRS branch office.

The Volunteer and Education Branch of the Internal
Revenue Service also offers free legal assistance if you get
audited. Privately supervised law and graduate accounting
school students are given special permission to practice

before the IRS on behalf of taxpayers who can't afford to hire a professional. Success rates have been surprisingly good! Contact the office at 202-566-6352 if you need this kind of help.

11 | *Business Assistance*

Tap Into Free Information Sources

One of the best things about our capitalist culture is that we all want to see businesses thrive and succeed. Successful business means gainful employment, a healthier economic pulse, and general prosperity. There are many dozens of systems installed throughout the nation to help insure your business does well. Most of these will answer your questions and work with you free of charge. Here is just a sampling:

US Small Business Administration
Hotline 800-827-5722

Contact these people to get the number of your local SBA affiliate. They can provide you with free advice and assistance on all kinds of situations that you might run into in your daily work, such as problems in accounting, marketing, or business planning.

Consumer Credit Counseling Service
Hotline 800-338-CCCS

If your business credit is in need of repair, these people can refer you to your local Cooperative Extension Service. The CES can, in turn, teach you how to fix your credit and get yourself up and running, free of charge.

Roadmap Program
U.S. Department of Commerce
14th & Constitution Ave., NW
Washington, D.C. 20230
Phone 202-377-3176

If treated with respect and patience, these people can provide information on virtually any aspect of starting and running any business.

Patents and Trademarks
US Department of Commerce
2121 Crystal Dr.
Arlington, Virginia 22202
Phone 703-557-3225

A $6.00 *Disclosure Statement* can protect your idea while you develop it and raise the money to patent it. The statement is good for up to two years as evidence of the date you conceived your invention. Call this office for more information on this, as well as on conducting your own patent and trademark searches, saving yourself hundreds or even thousands of dollars in legal fees.

Free Advice From Experts

At the push of a few buttons all the expert advice you could ever need can be made available to you, free of charge! There are hundreds of organizations and departments, associations and federations whose sole mission is to provide answers to those with questions. These are experts who have devoted years of education and commitment to learning their fields. If they can't answer your question, they will provide you with a lead to someone who can!

The following three offices can provide you with help in locating experts in both government and private sectors on just about anything you need to know about anything, including such things as grants between $5,000 and

$150,000! All information is free.

Government Sources
Federal Information Center
P.O. Box 600
Cumberland, Maryland 21501-0600
Phone 301-722-9000

Centers of this type are located throughout the country, where experts can be found on just about any topic.

Organizations and Associations
Information Central
American Society of Association Executives
1575 I St. NW
Washington, D.C. 20005

As we have discussed, affiliating yourself with those in your field who are successful and wealthy is the easiest route to personal success and wealth. Research the associations of interest to you or call these people and they will find it for you.

Technical Information
Science and Technology Division
Reference Section, Library of Congress
First and Independence, SE
Washington, D.C. 20540

Perhaps the most complete and accurate source of information in the world, the Library of Congress offers free information for the asking. Small fees may be charged if you wish the data to be hard copied and sent to you.

And here are but a few of many dozens of information resources and clearinghouses that can help you in business or any other type of research:

Agriculture and Commodities
Office of Public Affairs
US Department of Agriculture

Room 402A
Fourteenth and Independence Ave. SW
Washington, D.C. 20250
Phone 202-720-4623

A staff of research specialists is available to provide
specific answers or direct you to an expert in any
agriculture-related topic. The National Agricultural
Library (301-344-3755) serves as a massive information
resource center on this issue, and the National
Agriculture Statistics Service can provide contacts for
agricultural production, stocks, prices, and other data.

Arts and Entertainment
Performing Arts Library
John F. Kennedy Center
101 Independence Ave., SE
CIP Division Rm 542
Washington, D.C. 20540
Phone 202-416-8780

Working with the Library of Congress, this center offers
reference services on any aspect of the performing arts.

Best and Worst Companies
US Department of Commerce
Fourteenth and Constitution Ave., NW
Herbert C. Hoover Building
Washington, D.C. 20230
Phone 202-482-2000

Monitoring all major US industry, over a hundred experts
at this office can provide detailed information on
virtually any industry or company.

Demographics
Data Users Service Division
Bureau of the Census
Customer Service

Washington, D.C. 20233
Phone 301-763-4100

A good hunk of your tax dollars goes toward constructing a gigantic statistic dynamo. This data, culled from the most recent census, as well as national economic and industrial data, would cost you thousands were you to go to a market research firm. It's free to you if you ask specifically and politely.

Other Nations

Country Officers
US Department of State
2201 C Street NW
Washington, D.C. 20520
Phone 202-647-4000

Economic, political, and any other background on every country in the world is available at this center. Call and ask for the number of the country officer for the nation in which you are interested.

Health

National Health Information Center
P.O. Box 1133
Washington, D.C. 2013-1133
Phone 800-336-4797

Can provide you with leads, both public and private sector, on virtually any aspect of health concerns.

Part III
Creating Wealth

12 | *A Philosophy for Living Rich*

Opening Yourself to the Language of the Rich

As you continue down the road to fulfilling your personal vision of wealth, you are certain to discover that being rich is not only about having a lot of money. Wealth has a style, a way of being, a language, if you will. Learning that language, tuning your ear to its pitch and timbre, will give you a head start toward achieving your goals.

We have already discussed things like prudence, frugality, and the ability to see the system through the eyes of the rich. We know that they value hard work and hold as precious every penny they earn. We know that they look past glitz and glamour in order to find solid quality and good value for their dollar. And we know that they don't make "blind" purchases; rather, they ask questions, shun trends, look for long-term value, and discard what they really don't need.

But what about other aspects of their lives? How does wealth influence them as people? Which of their personal values change once they achieve wealth? And how can we take those values and employ them so we can better achieve our own visions right now, and not in some indefinite future?

Flamboyant, like Donald Trump, or conservative, like Lee Iacocca; immaculate, like Ted Turner, or disheveled, like any of those upstart computer magnates, the one thing that multi-millionaires all have in common is that they allow *richness* into their lives. These people value discovery. They see problems not as annoyances or setbacks, but as challenges. They have little use for fretting, since taking action resolves situations a whole lot faster than whining about them. Most of all, they utilize words and sentences in ways that make people listen to their ideas and stand by them when the going gets rough.

Wealthy people know that in order to stay ahead they have to take into consideration other points of view. This is how talent is recognized and discovered, how from small ideas big money comes. Absorb data, take an interest in culture, current events, economic developments, the arts; pay attention not just to the media but to the way the media works. This is the language of the rich! Then, don't just spout or parrot what you've learned. Filter it all through your own unique experience and practice expressing your opinions until you can do so comfortably.

Create a plan. Develop an idea. Find something that truly interests you and seek out role models who have attained great success doing what you want to do. Meet and understand these role models. Only then will you be able to successfully navigate in the circles of the wealthy. Of course, before any of this happens you must a have solid sense of dignity and self-worth.

You Are Worth a Lifetime's Income

Whether or not you are pure of heart and noble in spirit, if you measure your earnings from your first job to your retirement you are still worth at least your weight in gold! You are an earning machine, and it is important to let people know this. Hard work, concentration, focus, and the ability to take action on ideas are all characteristics that make you worthy of being wealthy. When wealth is accumulated, jobs are created the economy is stimulated, we feel a little more free to spend more. Any way you look at it, you simply *must* feel good about becoming wealthy!

Pursue wealth with passion, not obsession. Fanatics are unhappy people who are actually self-absorbed and greedy, as opposed to having something to offer. Wealthy people provide service. Believe it or not, much of their action is in giving! Consumers part with money because they feel, to some degree or another, they are getting some value. The richest people are giving others the best value for their money. (Every one of those M&M packs and Mars Bars comes with a money-back guarantee, after all!) Take this into consideration as you embark on your pursuit of wealth. You are worth it, especially when you make a meaningful commitment.

Give and You Shall Receive

Chalk it up to karma, divine justice, or the laws of physics, but give and you are most likely going to get back! It may not be as simple as an exchange at the cash register, but when you provide a service, when you do someone a favor, when you have given to a charitable cause, you have set something positive into the world that will not go unnoticed.

Giving something of yourself, with little expectation of getting anything in return, rests in the subconscious mind of the person you have given to. It lends a positive air to your personality and you will be appreciated in subtle ways. When you've given to someone, you are more likely to be listened to by that person. They will be more receptive to your ideas and more likely to do you favors. Give, and have patience. One day, you may ask for something completely out of left field—totally unreasonable—and watch what happens!

13 | *Networking*

Speaking in Wealthy Circles

Behind every wealthy person are dozens, if not hundreds, of people who put him or her there. Unless you hit the lottery or a jackpot somewhere, you're not going to get rich in a vacuum. You work five days a week at a small firm and someone gives you a meager pittance for a salary. Work the world seven days a week and someone is a lot more likely to provide you with wealth. To truly live rich, you are going to have to break out that Rolodex and rally the forces! Take names and numbers. Move yourself into a complex network of connections, acquaintances, and alliances. Penetrate those wealthy circles, and gain acceptance.

Six Degrees of Separation

"It's not *what* you know, it's *who* you know." The line has some credence. The less isolated you are, the more likely you are to be in contact with the kind of people who can help you become successful. Seek out people who are successful in one form or another. Connect with them. Ask questions and listen hard while they answer. People love to talk about themselves, and you can learn from what they have to say. Keep in mind that it's more than possible that any person you meet knows somebody who could make a big difference to your future. A famous playwright recently said that we are all connected to one another through six people at the most. For example, you may know someone who is quite friendly with someone whose brother is chummy with the financial attorney of the President of the United States! It's a smaller world than you think, and networking can traverse it quite quickly.

Presenting Your Package

There are many reasons why circulating among the rich can be a benefit to you. Studying, interacting with, and acclimating yourself toward wealthy people will give you a first-hand look at their values and experiences. Instead of settling for an abstract vision of what it would be like to be truly rich, you can encounter the benefits and drawbacks yourself by watching and speaking with them. You will also realize that these people are really no better or worse than you are. The glamour will start to fade after a while, and you will see that what sets them apart is merely their access to knowledge and how they utilize what other people don't know.

Nonetheless, it could be quite a task to approach one of these people. Economic boundaries could weigh heavily on both sides, with all the accompanying biases and prejudices. Your great ideas, your candidacy for a better job, your basic friendship could be ignored if you are too abrupt or wordy. If you are a package that is truly worth opening, you're going to need a quick lesson on presentation.

These easy steps can smooth out those first awkward moments and help you toward establishing a lasting connection:

1. Listen carefully! Just as you want certain things, so does everyone else. When we get those things, we become happy. We appreciate the people who bring us those things and we want to please them. That way, we can get more!

When you are truly listening to a person, you are observing not just their spoken words, but posture, mannerisms, behavioral tics. A man who keeps glancing over at your potato chips is probably hoping you'll offer him some. Offer him some chips, even if he refuses at first! Learning what the person you're listening to really wants, and then being able to provide it for him or her is half the battle!

People are always telling you what they want in little ways. Wealthy people tend to be more guarded, but they can be drawn out with polite questions and a keen ear. Listen, and with brief responses, show them that you understand what they are talking about. Listening, you will realize, is a precious ability.

2. Find out what you have in common. When you have common interests, likes, and dislikes, it becomes easier to guide a conversation in the direction you'd like it to go. Fortunately, human experience does not vary all that much. Respond to an anecdote with a brief story that places you in a similar dilemma. Show how you solved it. Share a bit of your knowledge about something that fascinates this person, then ask his or her opinion. Engage, share, and listen to what that person has to say, and you've begun to build a comfortable relationship.

3. Offer something free of charge. Once you've established common ground and figured out a little bit about what this person is looking for, offer something of yourself. This could be as simple as smiling or touching the person. Being touched creates intimacy and when done right can truly start a bond!

As we discussed in the section on barter, you could offer this person a skill, service, or connection that might contribute toward achieving a specific goal. Do this without necessarily asking or expecting something in return. This will most certainly gain you attention, and you will make a favorable impression. Be sure to deliver, however, or you will end up doing yourself a disservice. Honoring your commitments and keeping your word will invest you with an air of integrity, a valuable asset in fulfilling your ultimate goal!

4. Ask for something in return. Quite possibly the most difficult step to take is to ask for something back. Wealthy people know how to be unreasonable. They ask for favors, they aren't afraid to ask questions, they ask for what they know they deserve. People can be inconsiderate, absentminded, or just slow on the uptake. They need to be asked. The worst they can say is no, and that will leave you no worse off than you were before you asked.

Your request does not have to be immediate. Try not to let everything seem like an even swap. This can look cynical or self-serving. On the other hand, don't keep putting it off. Chances are, if what you wish to express is sitting on the tip of your tongue, taking action is your best bet. Ask. If it doesn't work out, rethink your approach, go back to step one, and start again.

Where to Go

Exclusivity is relative. Certainly there are big-ticket events that forbid most of us from hobnobbing with the likes of the rich and famous. Private parties are a case in point. Thousand-dollar-a-plate dinners should be left to those who can bathe in greenbacks and feel clean afterward. But there are several places you can go to network with wealthy people where the playing field is fairly even. Hobbies, interests, charities and culture are shared by all of us, rich or poor. Our love of team sports stretches across all economic boundaries. What follows are some other suggested areas for networking:

Trade Shows and Expos. The most likely places to network and establish connections, trade shows, conventions, and expositions gather dozens, perhaps thousands, of people under one roof who share the same interests, hobbies, professions and political goals. Forget the cliché that they're boring. You're not going there to disco the night away! Pull together some credentials, create your own business letterhead if you have to, but go to these events.

Listings and announcements for these types of shows are often buried in your local newspaper. Your best bet is to follow the trade publications in your areas of interest. Contact the organization running the show and make certain the subject matter and exhibition are going to be worth the price of admission. Try attending during the "trade" portion of the event, usually held on the first day or so, when consumers are not mobbing the area. Things are less frantic and the people you want to talk to have more free time. Once you get there, study the programs, attend the seminars, and fill that Rolodex. Then follow through with letters and phone calls to confirm your conversations and take action on your goals.

Cultural Events. Movers, shakers, and leaders keep high profiles at ethnic, religious, and international events, or other causes for public celebrations. While they may not be as easy to approach, contact can be made if you have a friendly disposition and a passionate interest in your cause.

Museums and Galleries. If your background is in history or the fine arts, museums, galleries, and other special exhibits may be the route to take. The more prepared you are, the more likely you'll be to break the ice and establish a firm contact. Read up on what you're going to see at the exhibit. Keep your ears open for general opinions about what is on display. Get caught without having done your homework, and the doors will slam shut on you.

Charity Functions. The secret to gaining access to any charity event can be summed up in one word: volunteer! You can contribute to a worthy cause by working hard and you won't have to part with cash. What could be better? But being a volunteer doesn't necessarily mean demeaning yourself, becoming a lowly gofer—someone to be ignored. Dress well. Handle your chores with poise and dignity. Interact with attendees respectfully, but with charm and liveliness. Don't be afraid to share ideas, and approach the people you need to talk with whenever the opportunity arises.

Select a charity that interests you. From the American Cancer Society to the American Zoological Society, foundations and charitable organizations are listed in your phone book and are on file at your local library. If the event is connected in some way with your goals, all the better!

Auction Houses. Contrary to their reputation for stuffiness, auction houses can be fascinating places, offering opportunities to see rare objects and antiquities of a kind you won't find in museums. Motion picture and sports memorabilia, animation cel art, doll miniatures, and antique toys are among the many items on display any given week. Anyone can get put on a mailing list. Do so, and go when something of interest turns up. Like-minded individuals, many of them quite wealthy, will be there.

Societies. Put away those evening gowns and tuxes; we're not talking about the posh society functions you read about in gossip columns. From Audobon and National Geographic, to the National Rifle Association and the Young Republicans, societies and associations are gathering places to share ideas and hopes. They assemble people with common social interests and actually make it conducive to pitch, network, and barter. These organizations can help you find a job or change the one you've got. They provide that ground of commonality you need to make your approach and the regularity to take that second shot if you need it.

Societies can cost some money to join, but contributions are often tax deductible and nearly all of them offer scholarships. Try to find several that match your interests, then join them. Study their publications and ask questions to avoid embarrassment. Be certain you understand what you're getting yourself into. Practice leadership skills by participating in the running of the organization. Become a familiar face with a friendly smile. Your attitude can result in a firm handshake; a distant possibility can become a reality.

14 | *Making Your Money Work for You*

A Dynamic Prospect

Wealthy people know that money is made in motion. Like huge turbines spinning out electricity or wheels spinning to propel a car, the circulation of cash generates interest, dividends, annuities—more cash!

Think of it this way: If you were to take the money you've saved through the recommendations in this book and stuff it in your mattress, it will never accrue any more. The money will remain static, not doing anything for you. Stash the same amount in a savings account, where it will be invested in large, sluggish, and highly conservative products, and your assets will earn a tiny bit of interest. But if you turn your attention toward stocks, mutual funds, variable annuities, and brand-new overseas investment opportunities, you have a dynamic prospect.

Generating Personal Insurance

In this day and age, the harsh realities of the national economy and employment rates must be faced before you invest the wealth you have accrued. While certain kinds of insurance—health and unemployment—are built into most jobs, it is strongly recommended that you hold onto your savings in the form of liquid assets until a respectable growth is generated. *Six to nine month's salary is not unreasonable* to have put aside as sort of personal insurance above and beyond whatever safeguards are built into your work. Do this before you start an overall investment portfolio.

The means and methods of saving money mentioned earlier in this book are perfect for setting aside this kind of savings, provided you adhere to your choice without wavering. In recent years, however, savings accounts have offered such low interest rates that there is little reason to utilize them to save this kind of money. Generating amounts of $100 to $300 in your checking account to then be sent into a high-yield mutual fund or variable annuity would seem to be the way to go. Your money will continue to move rapidly in these accounts, reinvesting itself and generating respectable dividends while still being liquid enough to get at quickly should the need arise.

And should you become unemployed or encounter some kind of health crisis, this money will act as a buffer, a distinct, "rainy day" savings not to be confused with your general investment portfolio, which should remain untouched and hard at work generating wealth, even during such an emergency.

Choosing an Investment Broker

Investing your hard-earned money is one area where discount houses and doing-it-yourself cannot be recommended. If you needed to have surgery, would you run to the kitchen, grab a knife, and flip open a medical book? The analogy is apt. When the economy was more stable, it may have been more lucrative to use discount brokers. But now… General Motors? U.S. Steel? IBM? In many ways "blue chip" stocks don't exist any more. There is no such thing as a "sure thing." Get hold of a professional!

You should pick an investment broker the same way you

choose a doctor or a lawyer. Seek out successful people and get their recommendations. Keep your ears open at those social functions or association meetings. Sit down with prospective investment brokers and ask questions. Make certain you are absolutely confident in this person's skills, and watch that you are being treated with respect!

A good investment broker will have a computer monitor on his or her desk from which information can be accessed in a matter of seconds. The world of finance is extremely unpredictable, with price fluctuations occurring from one minute to the next based on anything from political decisions made half way around the world to natural disasters. From that screen, choices can be made and changed instantly. Do not settle for less! The brokerage firm you choose should also have people on the floor of the New York Stock Exchange, so that these decisions may be implemented as soon as possible at the source.

The Stock Market and Mutual Funds

Like a doctor or lawyer, your stock broker will want to know what your goals are so that he or she can act in your best interest. Your age, income, risk tolerance, cash flow, net worth, and investment time horizon are all important factors in how your broker will help you create wealth.

Knowing that you wish to build wealth, your broker will probably recommend a mixture of products on the rise on the New York or American Stock Exchange, or NASDAQ, as well as mutual funds. Playing the stock market might be construed as educated gambling. The object: to buy a stock when it is low priced and has the potential to rise steadily over the course of time and to sell it when it fulfills that potential.

Many people will avoid investing in stocks, fearing some kind of market crash. This is nonsense. Investors and brokers who lost their shirts and flung themselves from high places during memorable "crashes" are people who tied enormous quantities of money up in highly volatile investments from which guarantees were made without the paper to back them. If a basic investment is solid, a few months' wait will see stock prices rise from the ashes. Of all investments made near the beginning of this century (including bonds and treasury bills), stocks are the products which have generated the most wealth and the highest upside potential. After you have saved several months' income (including salary and those dollars and pennies, nickels and dimes you've saved by slashing your spending), it is recommended that you generate an additional $5,000 before you start investing in stocks.

Mutual funds are actually collections of stock purchases, also know as "stock portfolios." Management companies which oversee mutual funds (such as Fidelity, Kemper, Prudential, or Dreyfus) invest your money in a variety of highly active stocks and other investment programs, and keep trading to generate profits as they fall and rise. Fees are set by how successful a given fund is doing currently. Generally speaking, mutual funds are a safer investment than an individual stock since your money is spread over dozens, even hundreds of individual stocks. And some mutual funds allow you to start with as little an investment as $250.

Variable Annuities

Variable annuity investment plans are tax-deferred, flexible payment annuities issued by such companies as Prudential and Merrill Lynch. Variable annuities allow you to choose from a variety of investment options, usually mixing traditional tax-deferred annuities with the timely investment opportunities of mutual funds. This offsets a healthy portion of taxation when you liquidate. A minimum $1,000 initial payment is invested and kept active in your choice of aggressive or conservative possibilities with no initial service fee.

Trading on Your IRA

Contributions to a retirement plan are tax deductible and not taxed as current income. Individual retirement accounts (IRAs) lay the groundwork toward a future that is financially secure and are vital for insuring a comfortable lifestyle later on. New developments in banking and investment brokering now allow you to activate your IRA in such a way as to enable you to trade on the money you've accrued without having to pay tax on capital gains. Ask your banker or investment broker about these services and take advantage of them.

Getting Rich With Upside Potential

As we move rapidly toward the turn of the century, a sweeping look back can provide us with both insight and a final clue as to what to do with the money we have worked so hard to save and invest. Turning our attention to a twenty-year span stretching from 1977 to 1997, the following chart will give you a sense of how inflation affects us as prices in general continue to rise with no signs of truly abating:

	1977	1987	(projected) 1997
One Family Home	$54,000	$115,290	$245,000
Gas Bill (Per Day)	$0.64	$1.04	$1.70
Electricity (Per Day)	$0.27	$0.57	$1.27
Paperback Novel	$1.99	$4.95	$6.95

But the news is not all grim. While it is true that prices will continue to rise, it is also true that certain types of investments will inevitably climb with them. If you take a look at three of the classic investment tools over the course of several decades, you will quickly notice that one of them has a direct correlation to this type of inflation. One of these three has the kind of upside potential that can stave off the agony of inflation, simply because its flexibility and sensitivity to what exactly is going on in the world keeps it viable. Take a look at the following chart:

	1925 Initial Investment	1993 Current Yield
Treasury Bills	$100	$ 225
Bonds	$100	$ 1,175
Stocks	$100	$15,000

Based on an investment of only $100 (with absolutely no additional investments), we see an increase in the average treasury bill of 125 percent over the course of nearly seventy years. This takes into account things like wars, recessions, government stability, and various economic factors. The same investment in the bond market makes for a significantly higher yield (1,175 percent), but the results of a one-hundred-dollar investment in the average, solid stock places the total yield at 15,000 percent! What if that person had made a stock investment on a monthly basis? Well, what if you did so, starting right now?

The stock market (and mutual investment funds that take advantage of aggressive stocks) is ultimately the shortest route to the greatest upside potential—a steady creation of wealth. After all, what are most stocks but investments in the very products whose prices keep rising year after year!

A good investment broker will steer you toward quality stocks which will rise with the times. Regular, monthly investments of the cash you've been saving through any number of the 81 ways shown you in this book can make you rich, no matter what your current income.

Index